CW00970936

GALASHIELS TO EDINBURGH

Roger Darsley & Dennis Lovett

Series Editor Vic Mitchell

Front cover picture: The RCTS West Riding Tour travelled over the Waverley Route on the 5th January 1969. Class 55 Deltic Co-CoDE no.9007 Pinza *hauled the train throughout from Leeds via Edinburgh returning via the East Coast Main Line back to Leeds. It was captured at Fountainhall during a photo stop. The last scheduled trains ran on Saturday 4th January.(G.W.Morrison)*

Top back cover picture - Class B1 4-6-0 no.61396 descends Falahill in June 1965. (KMF/ARPT)

Lower back cover picture - Class 17 Bo-BoDE no.D8554 enters Millerhill in March 1965. (Colour Rail)

Readers of this book may be interested in the following societies:

North British Railway Study Group
c/o R.W.Lynn,
2, Brecken Court, Saltwell Road South,
Low Fell, Gateshead,
NE9 6EY
www.nbrstudygroup.co.uk

Railway Correspondence and Travel Society, Scottish Branch
℅ Mr R. Thornburn,
2 Tryst Park, Hunters Tryst, Fairmilehead,
Edinburgh, EH10 7RD
www.rcts.org.uk

Waverley Route Heritage Association
Signal Box cottage, Whitrope,
Hawick, Roxburghshire, TD9 9TY
www.wrha.org.uk

Old Gala Club
Secretary Mrs Helen Elliott,
19 Wedale, Stow, Galashiels, TD1 2SJ
www.oldgalaclub.org.uk

Published December 2013

ISBN 978 1 908174 52 9

Design Deborah Esher

Published by
Middleton Press
Easebourne Lane
Midhurst
West Sussex
GU29 9AZ
Tel: 01730 813169
Fax: 01730 812601
Email: info@middletonpress.co.uk
www.middletonpress.co.uk

Printed in the United Kingdom by Henry Ling Limited, Dorset Press, Dorchester. DT1 1HD

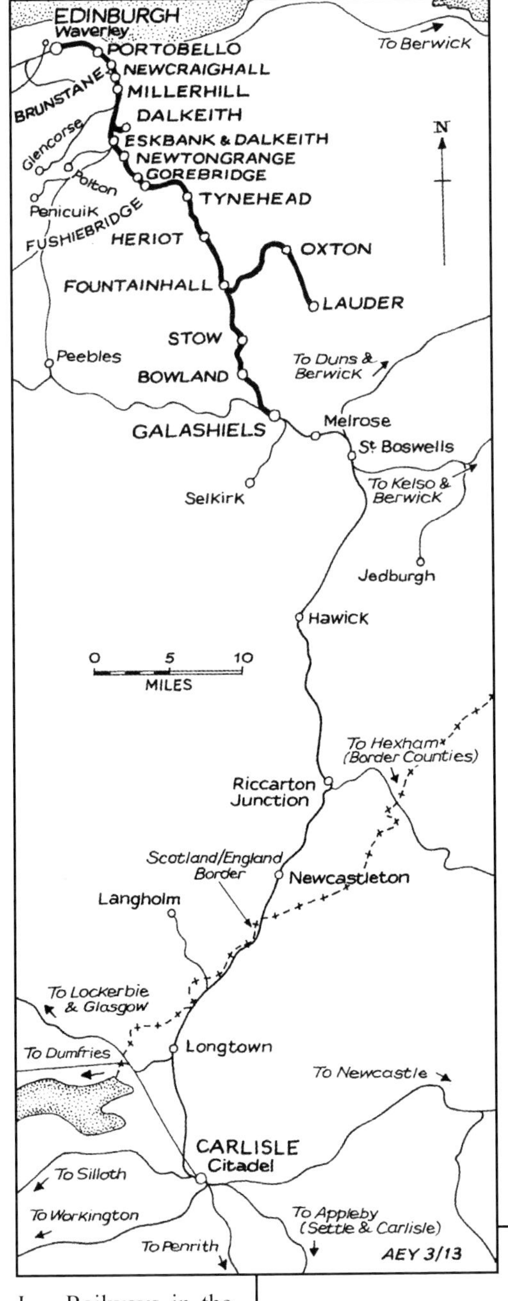

I. Railways in the area in 1922 with later stations added. (A.E.Young)

INDEX

ACKNOWLEDGEMENTS

We are grateful for the assistance received from many of those mentioned in the photographic credits and also to G.Croughton, J.P.McCrickard, A.P.McLean, V.Mitchell, J.W.Yellowlees (First ScotRail) and Mrs N.Darsley.

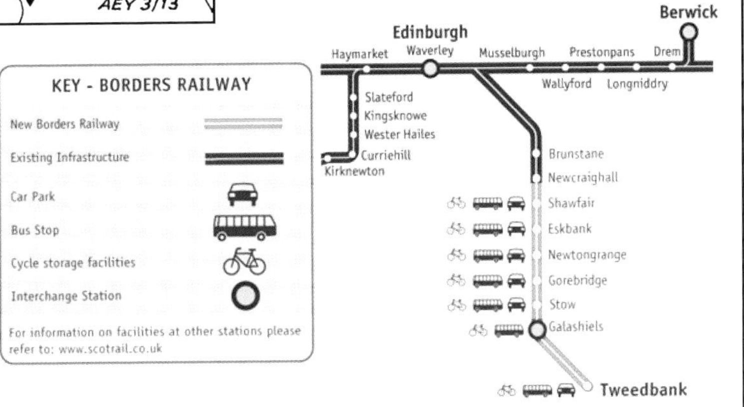

II. Map showing the section of the Waverley Route to be reopened in 2015

GEOGRAPHICAL SETTING

From Galashiels to Fountainhall, the line followed the Gala Water which it crossed some 15 times whilst ascending the narrow valley. On leaving Galashiels the first major engineering feat was Bowshank Tunnel (249 yards) which takes the line through Bowshank Hill. Today the abandoned, but soon to be reinstated trackbed, Gala Water and the A7 trunk road follow the same contours in very close proximity to each other all the way to Heriot. At Heriot the Heriot Water joins the Gala Water from their respective sources before the railway's final climb to Falahill.

North of Galashiels, the railway crosses the Silurian and Ordovician strata of the Moorfoot Hills, the catchment area for both the Gala Water and, to the west, the River Tweed.

Once over the watershed at Tynehead, there are two major faults that lead to the Carboniferous strata of the Lothian coalfield and the valleys of the Rivers, Tyne, Esk and North Esk. The coalfield starts at Fushiebridge.

The surface area of the Lothian coalfield was sculptured by the retreat to the east of the last ice age and pitted for the last three hundred years by the pits and heaps of the coal workings. Limestone has also been worked in the past but not as extensively as coal.

At Falahill the line bisects the narrow gap between the Moorfoot Hills to the West, where the Gala Water rises and the Lammermuir Hills to the East. Falahill is the highest point on the line between Hawick and Edinburgh at 880ft above sea level. Its gradients required the use of banking locomotives in steam days which worked north from Galashiels and south from Hardengreen.

From Falahill the line descends to the Midlothian coalfield and then skirts to the east of the Pentland Hills. Two other major rivers have to be crossed on the journey north, firstly the River South Esk which rises in the Moorfoot Hills and was crossed after leaving Newtongrange, requiring the building of the 22 arch Newbattle Viaduct (also known as Lothian Bridge). Likewise the River North Esk which rises in the Pentland Hills had to be crossed between Eskbank and Sheriffhall stations and resulted in the building of a further major viaduct.

The impressive volcanic rocks on which both Edinburgh Castle and Arthur's Seat sit, dictate that the railway takes a circuitous route to join the East Coast Main Line at Portobello.

In Edinburgh, the site of the current Waverley station and the neighbouring Princes Street Gardens, was in the early part of the 18th century occupied by the Nor Loch. Due to overcrowding in the old town, the Nor Loch had become a stinking cess pool and in 1759 a decision was taken to drain it. It was gradually infilled and by 1820 had created a link between the old town around the castle and the new town being developed to the north of Princes Street. This area was to provide the land for the world famous Princes Street Gardens and through which Edinburgh's railway lines would eventually converge.

Fountainhall – Lauder

Lauder was served by a 10¼ mile branch from Fountainhall which crossed the Moorfoot Hills to enter Lauderdale. The line left its junction with the main line and rose at 1 in 50 to cross the Gala Water and then the main Edinburgh – Galashiels road (now the A7) by means of a level crossing. Steadily rising the line followed the Nethertoun Burn to Middletoun and at the 2½ milepost reached a height of 944 ft above sea level. The line then followed the Mean Burn from its source to Threeburnford where it crossed the road from Oxton by two level crossings before passing Airhouse Quarry which provided regular rail traffic to the line until its closure in the 1950s. The line then descended to Oxton before entering Lauderdale and following the valley of the Leader Water to terminate on the northern edge of the Berwickshire town.

Glenesk Junction – Dalkeith

A half mile long branch line left the Waverley route at Glenesk Junction to reach the town of Dalkeith. Beyond Dalkeith the Duke of Buccleuch owned collieries at Smeaton and Cowden. To link these to the Dalkeith branch a private tramway was constructed and included a major wooden viaduct known as 'Victoria' over the River South Esk. From the station at Dalkeith to the outskirts of the town at Elmfield it ran through the streets before continuing on its own alignment to Thorneybank. Here the line separated with one line heading to Smeaton and the other to Cowden. The collieries around Smeaton were known as Dalkeith Collieries, although they were some distance from the town.

The building of an alternative route from Hardengreen Junction to Smeaton resulted in the tramway section being abandoned from 31st July 1870.

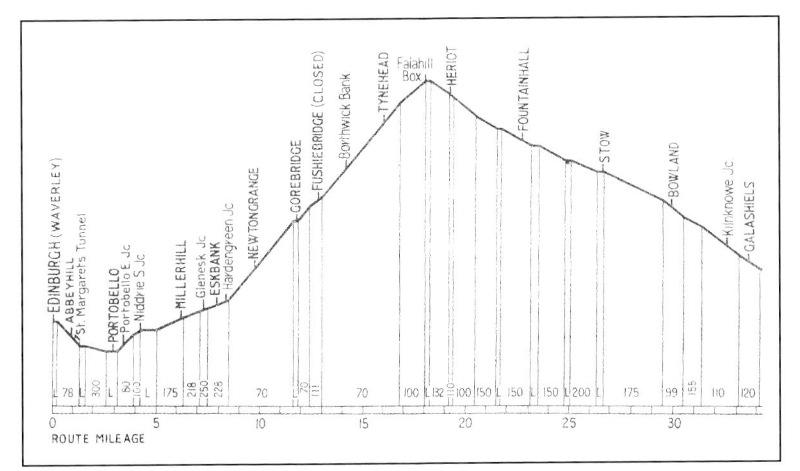

Edinburgh - Galashiels

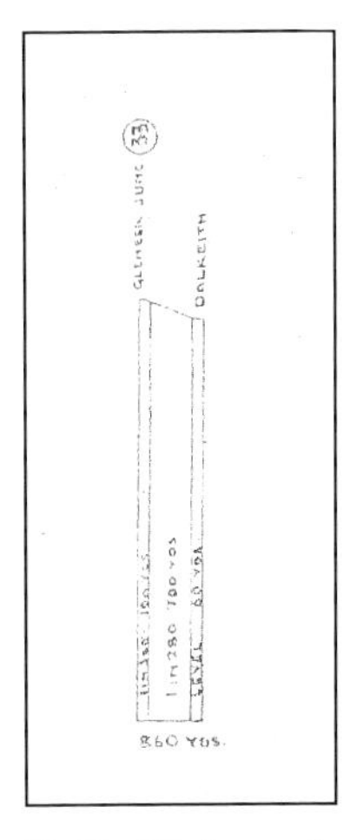

Dalkeith branch

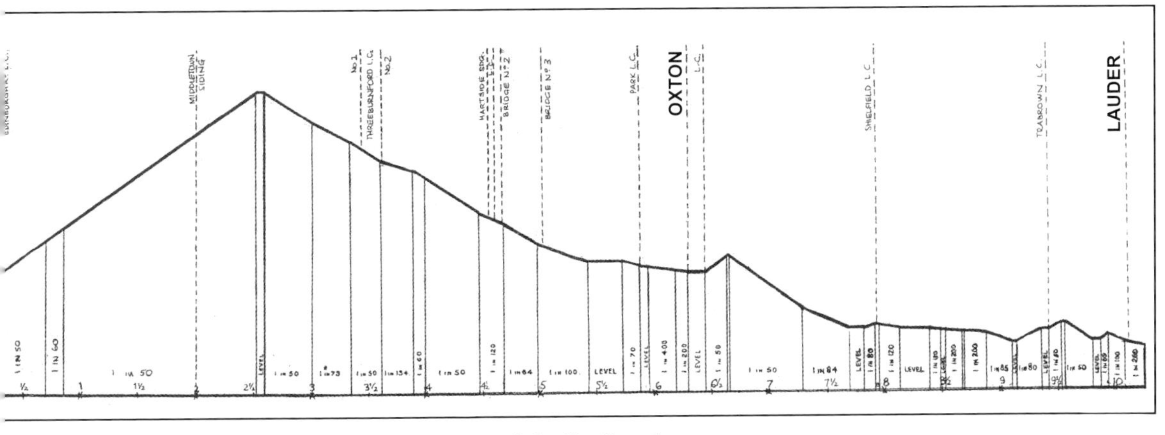

Fountainhall – Lauder

HISTORICAL BACKGROUND

The first section of line from Edinburgh to Dalkeith was built to feed Edinburgh's enormous appetite for coal. Edinburgh was not called 'Auld Reekie' by Sir Walter Scott for any other reason that the sky above it was filled with smoke from its many chimneys.

To the south east of Edinburgh lay the Lothian coalfield. In the early part of the 19th century the primitive roads were often impassable for long periods during the harsh winters. Whilst coal could be delivered from the Lanarkshire coal fields via the Forth & Clyde Canal (opened 1790) and the Union Canal which branched off at Falkirk to serve the capital city (opened 1820) they too became unusable when they froze and the coal barges were stranded often for several weeks. Even sea borne traffic into Leith became difficult in winters which were much harsher than they are today.

The desire to build a waggonway was first discussed in 1817 but came to nothing. However, in 1824 a meeting of interested parties agreed to proceed with a line from Dalhousie (later known as South Esk) to a terminus in the city at St. Leonards located in the shadow of the famous Edinburgh landmark of Arthur's Seat. St. Leonards was accessed through a 572 yards tunnel. Thanks to the support of a number of land owners an Act of Parliament was obtained on 26th May 1826. Built at a cost of £120,000 the line ran from St. Leonard's through Niddrie, Cairney, Millerhill, Sheriffhall and Eskbank. Niddrie emerged as the hub of the network with branches to the harbour at Fisherrow (opened 1831) and Leith (opened 1838).

At the south end of the line a number of private waggonways connected to the mainline which were all built to the Scotch Gauge of 4ft 6ins. It used horse haulage throughout its independent existence. The main line crossed the River North Esk on a 60ft viaduct but the engineers did not take the challenge of crossing the River South Esk and the line terminated at Dalhousie on the river's north bank.

One major landowner was the Marquess of Lothian whose mines lay south of the Dalhousie terminus. In order to gain maximum benefit from the existing line, he decided to fund an extension to the south to access his pits at Arniston near Gorebridge which had opened in 1832. In order to reach Arniston, it was necessary to cross the River South Esk. As a result of the high cost of building this structure (later rebuilt and still standing as Newbattle Viaduct) the Marquess was allowed to convey his coal free of charge over the North Esk Viaduct.

The Duke of Buccleuch also constructed a viaduct across the River South Esk when he built an extension of the Dalkeith branch (opened 1838) which left the main line at Glenesk, just south of the North Esk viaduct.

The Edinburgh & Hawick Railway was planned as a single track railway to the inherited 4ft 6ins Scotch gauge and gained Parliamentary approval in 1845. It utilised the existing Edinburgh & Dalkeith and the Marquess of Lothian's waggonway. Before work began, the new Edinburgh & Hawick Railway was acquired by the North British Railway (NBR) with the route being upgraded to double track and built to the British Standard Gauge of 4ft 8½ ins with the existing route converted accordingly. The Edinburgh terminus was also changed to that of North Bridge, terminus of the NBR line from Berwick (later Berwick-upon-Tweed) which had opened in June 1846. North Bridge was renamed Waverley in April 1866.

The line opened in sections; to Dalhousie on 21st June 1847, Gorebridge on 14th July 1847 and to Fountainhall on 4th May 1848. The line south of Galashiels can be found in our *Carlisle to Hawick* and *Hawick to Galashiels* albums.

On completion the line became known as the Waverley Route taking its name from the Waverley Novels by Sir Walter Scott, whose home was at Abbotsford near Melrose.

The 33½ miles long line from Galashiels to Edinburgh was elevated into a main line from 1862 by the opening of the Carlisle – Hawick section, although that section at first was a major financial drain on the NBR who considered selling or closing it. The arrival of the Midland Railway (MR) in Carlisle in 1876 provided the NBR with a partner, enabling through Anglo-Scottish services from London (St. Pancras).

In 1923 the NBR became part of the Scottish Area of the London & North Eastern Railway (LNER), the latter passing to the new British Railways, Scottish Region (BR, Sc.R) created upon nationalisation in 1948.

With closure of the remaining branch lines in the 1960s it was not long before the main line itself was threatened. Despite a belated fight by objectors, the last passenger trains ran on 5th January 1969, with freight lasting just a few months longer. A further attempt to save the line by a new Border Union company also sadly failed, track lifting being completed south of Newtongrange (Lady Victoria Pit) in 1972. For many years the trackbed was protected but road improvements in Galashiels, on the A7 at Falahill and the building of the Edinburgh by-pass all threatened any reopening plans.

The Border towns never really accepted the closure of the line which they had fought hard to retain and campaigns began to link the declining industrial towns with a buoyant jobs market in Edinburgh. With transport capacity from the North, West and East of the capital already fully stretched it gave further impetus to reopen the northern end of the Waverley route. The first significant move saw the reopening of the remaining section of the line to Millerhill to passenger trains to serve new stations at Brunstane and Newcraighall, thus extending the Edinburgh suburban routes to the south of the city. Passenger services began on the 3rd June 2002.

Borders Rail Futures and the Campaign for Borders Rail had by 2000 developed a strong case for reopening the line to Galashiels and later to the new town of Tweedbank (located 1½ miles from Melrose). By 2003 the campaign had reached the Scottish Government who finally assumed responsibility for rail issues in Scotland from Westminster in 2005. On 14 June 2006 the campaign received the go-ahead in an historic 114-1 vote, with Royal Assent granted the following month on 24 July.

Fountainhall – Lauder

There were proposals as early as 1846 to include the Berwickshire town of Lauder in the developing rail network but despite several proposals nothing materialised. The passing of the Light Railways Act of 1896 however, finally allowed the town's ambitions to be materialised with the construction of a 10 mile long light railway to join the Waverley Route at Fountainhall.

Promoted by two local landowners it opened on 2nd July 1901 and was worked by the NBR from the outset. Traffic was mainly passengers to and from Edinburgh and freight was mainly agricultural. An intermediate station was provided at Oxton, four miles from the Lauder terminus.

Improvements to the main road (now the A68) through the town and the rapid expansion of the bus operator who started a direct service from Lauder to Edinburgh in 1924, to Jedburgh in 1927 and to Newcastle-upon-Tyne in 1928. This resulted in a major loss of passenger traffic and the passenger service closed on 12th September 1932.

The line, like many in the Borders, was closed by flooding on 12th August 1948 and did not reopen until 20th November 1950.

The line remained open for freight traffic until 30th September 1958 but was visited by a Branch Line Society special train on 15th November 1958. Track lifting commenced in late 1960 and was completed the following year with the exception of a section retained as a shunting spur at Fountainhall.

Glenesk Junction - Dalkeith

The Edinburgh & Dalkeith Railway stopped short of Dalkeith due to the need to cross the River South Esk and terminated initially on the north bank at Dalhousie when it opened on 4th July 1831.

A new line just half a mile long to the centre of the town was opened at 4ft 6ins gauge line on 26th November 1838 from a junction at Glenesk. It was closed for re-gauging to standard gauge between June and July 1847.

In 1862 the North British Railway received the Royal Assent for a three mile line from Hardengreen Junction to be built to Smeaton. This avoided the need to traverse the streets of Dalkeith but utilised the existing route from the Victoria Viaduct to Smeaton. The original section between the viaduct, which was rebuilt and the passenger terminus at Dalkeith was abandoned with the opening of the new line on 31st July 1870.

This line was closed like many others temporarily during World War 1 between 1st January 1917 and 1st October 1919 but finally closed to passengers on 5th January 1942. Freight services ceased on 10th August 1964. The station site was a bus station and depot operated by First Group until 2011, when the site was redeveloped.

PASSENGER SERVICES

The 1910 timetable showed 11 through trains between Hawick and Edinburgh, four of which were worked in conjunction with the Midland Railway and originated and terminated at London St. Pancras and included an overnight sleeper service.

The 1922 timetable had 10 trains in the Down direction from Hawick to Edinburgh, three of which were through trains from London St. Pancras including the overnight sleeper which left Carlisle at 04.33 and two which began at Hawick. A through train operated from Newcastle via the Border Counties line leaving Newcastle at 16.27 joining the Waverley route at Riccarton Junction at 18.50. The Up direction was served by 11 trains from Edinburgh to Hawick including three workings to London St. Pancras and four local workings to Hawick. There were additional trains at 13.03 and 17.34 to Gorebridge.

The final timetable for the route (from 6th May 1968 until closure on 5th January 1969) had 11 workings in each direction, of which 3 down and 3 up trains served London St. Pancras including the overnight sleeper service. Of the remaining 8 workings, 3 ran to and from Carlisle, 3 to and from Hawick and the remaining two trains provided a commuter service from Eskbank & Dalkeith in the morning and in the late afternoon. This train, the 17.11 from Edinburgh Waverley, terminated at Gorebridge before forming the 18.03 from Eskbank & Dalkeith return working.

Lauder Branch

On opening in 1901 four passenger trains a day in each direction were provided. This was reduced to 3 each way after the end of World War 1. During the hostilities the service was reduced to 2 trains per day. At the time of closure the service was still 3 trains a day and after closure, the line continued to see excursion and special trains.

Dalkeith Branch

The 1922 timetable showed three trains per day operating in each direction between Edinburgh Waverley and Dalkeith serving Abbeyhill, Piershill, Portobello and Millerhill. Journey time was 22 minutes.

DALKEITH AND HAWICK BRANCH.—North British.

Mls	Down.	1 2 3 gov.	1 2 3 clss.	1 2 3 class.	1 2 3 clss.	1 2 3 clss.	1 2 3 clss.	1 2 3 clss.	1 2 3 clss.	Fares. 1 cl.	Fares. 2 cl.
	From North Bdg. St.	mrn	mrn	morn	noon	aft	aft.	*	aft	s. d.	s. d.
	Edinburgh dep.	8 15	8 45	10†45	12 0	2 0	3 45	4 30	8 15	..	..
3	Portobello	8 23	8 53	10 53	12 8	2 8	3 53	4 38	8 23	0 6	0 4
4½	Niddrie	8 30	9 0	11 0	1215	2 15	4 0	4 45	8 30	0 8	0 6
8	Dalkeith	..	9 10	..	1225	2 25	4 10	..	8 40	1 0	0 9
8	Gallowshall	8 38	..	11 8	..	..	..	4 53	..	1 0	0 9
9	Dalhousie	8 41	..	11 11	..	..	..	4 56	..	1 2	0 10
12	Gorebridge	8 51	..	11 21	..	..	..	5 6	..	1 9	1 4
16	Tyne-Head	9 5	..	11 35	..	..	..	5 20	..	3 0	2 0
19½	Heriot	9 15	..	11 45	..	..	..	5 30	..	3 9	2 9
22¾	Fountainhall	9 25	..	11 55	..	..	..	5 40	..	4 6	3 4
27	Stow	9 37	..	12 7	..	..	..	5 52	..	5 6	4 0
30	**Bowlnd. Brdg.**	9 45	..	12 15	..	..	..	6 0	..	6 0	4 4
33½	Galashiels	9 55	..	12 25	..	..	..	6 10	..	7 0	5 0
37½	Melrose	10 5	..	12 35	..	..	..	6 20	..	8 0	5 9
40¼	N. Town, St. Boswls.	1015	..	12 45	..	..	..	6 30	..	8 6	6 3
45½	New Belses	1030	..	1 0	..	..	..	6 45	..	9 6	7 0
53	**Hawick** arr.	1050	..	1 20	..	..	..	7 5	..	11 0	8 6

Up.	1 2 3 gov.	1 2 3 clss.	1 2 3 clss.	1 2 3 class.	1 2 3 clss.	1 2 3 clss.	1 2 3 clss.	1 2 3 clss	1 2 3 clss.
	mrn	mrn	mrn	morn	aft	aft	aft	aft	aft.
Hawick dep	7* 0	..	..	10 † 0	..	..	..	3†30	..
New Belses	7 20	..	..	10 20	..	..	..	3 50	..
N. Town, St. Boswls.	7 35	..	..	10 35	..	..	..	4 5	..
Melrose	7 44	..	..	10 44	..	..	..	4 14	..
Galashiels	7 55	..	..	10 55	..	..	..	4 25	..
Bowlnd. Brdg.	8 5	..	..	11 5	..	..	..	4 35	..
Stow	8 13	..	..	11 13	..	..	..	4 43	..
Fountainhall	8 23	..	..	11 25	..	..	..	4 55	..
Heriot	8 32	..	..	11 35	..	..	..	5 5	..
Tyne Head	8 42	..	..	11 45	..	..	..	5 15	..
Gorebridge	8 52	..	..	11 57	..	..	..	5 25	..
Dalhousie	9 0	..	..	12 5	..	..	..	5 33	..
Gallowshall	9 3	9 20	11 0	12 10	1 0	3 0	4 30	5 36	9 0
Dalkeith	..	9 20	11 0	..	1 0	3 0	4 30	..	9 0
Niddrie	9 13	9 30	1110	12 20	1 10	3 10	4 40	5 46	9 10
Portobello	9 20	9 37	1117	12 27	1 17	3 17	4 47	5 52	9 17
Edinburgh arr.	9 30	9 45	1125	12 35	1 25	3 25	4 55	6 0	9 25

Extra.—Edinburgh to Dalkeith—At 10 morn. * Stop at Fushie Bridge and Newstead. † Stop at Hassendeen.

On SUNDAYS.—Edinburgh to Hawick, at 8¾ morn. and 5 aft. Hawick to Edinburgh, at 8¾ morn. and 5 aft.

Edinburgh to Musselburgh.—At 9¼ and 11¼ morn., 1, 3, 4 40, 7, and 9¼ aft.

Musselburgh to Edinburgh.—At 8½, 9¾, and 11¾ morn.; 2, 4, 6, and 8¾ aft.

Edinburgh to Portobello.—At 8, 8¼, 8¾, 9¼, 10, 10¾, 11¼ morn., & 12 noon; 1, 2, 2½, 3, 3¾, 4, 4½, 4 40, 7, 8¼ and 9¼ aft.

Portobello to Edinburgh.—At 8 40, 8 50, 9 20, 9 35, 9 40, 9 58, 11¼, & 11 55 morn.; 12 5, 12 25, 1 15, 2 10, 3¼, 4 10, 4¾, 5 50, 6 10, 7¼, 8 25, and 9¼ aft.

The 1850 timetable showing services to the termini at Dalkeith and Hawick. The line south of Hawick to Carlisle did not open until 1862. This resulted in the up and down lines changing over.

CARLISLE, RIDDINGS, RICCARTON, HAWICK, ST. BOSWELLS, GALASHIELS, and EDINBURGH.—North British.

Miles from Carlisle	St. Pancras Station,	aft		aft	mrn	mrn	ngt	mrn	aft	mrn	aft	aft	aft	mrn	mrn	aft	mrn	aft	aft	aft	aft	SUNDAYS aft	mrn	aft	aft
	London 480 ..dep.	9 15					12 0			5 15					9 30		1130				1 30	9h15			
	360 " (Euston) "	8 50		1150			1150			5 15							1015					8h50			
	646 M'chester (Vic) "	mrn								9 55				9 55	1240		1 35					mrn			
	434 " v. Tyldesley "	1 0												10 2	1230	g	2 5					1 0			
	664 " v. Hellifield "	1240								9 30					1220		2 25				4 40	1240			
	442 Liverpool* 440 "	1245		mrn			mrn			9 40					1150		1 55					1245			
	680 " (Exchange) "			2 35			2 35			10 5				10 5	1 0		2 25								
	680 " v. Hellifield "	1235								9 30					1235		2 20				4 35	1235			
	Preston 418 .. "	2 23		3 20			3 20			11 5				11 5	1 55		3 21					2 23			
	Sheffield 481 "	1238	a	1 10	a		1 58			9 0					1217		2 5				4 0	1238			
	544 Leeds, Wellingtn "	1 i 0		2 i 5			4 4			10 5					1 28		3 30				5 33	1 0			
	Bradford 544 "	1 i 5		1 i 5						8 55					1250	v	2 55				5 0	1 5			
	Citadel Station,	mrn		mrn	mrn	mrn	mrn	mrn	aft	aft	aft	aft	aft	aft	aft	aft	aft	aft	aft	aft	aft	mrn	mrn	aft	aft
—	Carlisle ....dep.	4 20		6 0			8 25			1 12				3 0	3 50		6 5			7 35	8 2	4 20			
—	Silloth 692..dep.									1115							4 35			4 35					
4¼	Harker			6 10			8 35							3 10						7 46					
6¾	Lyneside			6 15			8 40							3 15						7 51					
9¼	Longtown 699			6 21			8 48		1240	1 27				3 22						7 59					
12	Scotch Dyke						8 53		1246					3 28						8 5					
14	Riddings 692			Stop			9 0		1253	1 36				3 34						8 11					
16¾	Penton						9 8		1 1					3 42											
21¼	Kershope Foot						9 18		1 11					3 52											
24¾	Newcastleton						9 26		1 19	1 54				4 0			6 39								
28¾	Steele Road						9 33		1 31					4 12											
32¾	Riccarton 693 arr.						9 48		1 41					4 22											
	Riccarton 693 dep.						9 51		1 48					4 45		6 26									
38¾	Shankend						10 4		Th.					4 59											
41½	Stobs			mrn			1011		2 4					5 6											
45¼	Hawick	5 32		6 0	6 55		1023		2 11	2e31		2 38		5 18		6 45	7o14		7 24		9 7	5 32	7 50	5 55	
49¾	Hassendean				7 4		1033					2 48		5 28					7 32				7 59	6 4	
53	Belses			6 14	7 12		1041					2 56		5 36					7 39				8 7	6 12	
57¾	St. Boswells 688, 692a	f		6 24	7 21		1050					3 5		5 45					7 47				8 17	6 22	
69¼	Kelso 692 ... arr.	7 5		7 5	9 0		1150					4 9		6 18					9 15				1017	7 9	
99¾	Berwick 689 "				1044		1 14					6 43		8g50											
—	St. Boswells .....dep.			6 28	7 24		1056				2 27	3 11		5 52				7 42	7 50				8 20	6 25	
61	Melrose			6 36	7 32	9 15	11 4			2e33	2 35	3 19		6 0			7o36	7 50	7 58		m		8 28	6 33	
64¾	Galashiels 692 arr.	5 58		6 43	7 39	9 21	1111			3 0	3 45	3 26		6 9			7 43	7 57	8 5		9 35	5 58	8 35	6 40	
	Galashiels 692 dep.	6 1		6 50	7 42	9 25	1116	1145		3 5		3 29		6 15			7 46	8 0			9 37	6 1	8 38	6 43	
68¼	Bowland			7 0				1155				3 39		6 25									8 48	6 53	
71¾	Stow, for Lauder			7 8	7 58			12 3				3 47		6 34				8 13					8 57	7 2	
75¾	Fountainhall 692			7 18	8 7			1213				3 56		6 44				TuS					9 7	7 12	
79	Heriot			7 27	8 18			1222				4 5		6 53									9 16	7 21	
82¼	Tynehead			7 36				1231				4 13		7 2									9 24	7 29	
85¼	Fushiebridge			7 45				1240				4 21		7 9									9 32	7 37	
86¾	Gorebridge			7 48	8 28			1243				4 24	6 15	7 12				8 38					9 35	7 40	7 50
89¼	Dalhousie ..[705, 693			7 56				1251				4 32	6 22	7 20									9 43		7 58
90¾	Eskbank, for Dalkeith			8 0	8 36	1058		1255				4 36	6 26	7 25				8 45					9 47	[illegible]	[illegible]
92	Millerhill 695...[705			8 5								4 41	6 38	7 31									9 52	[illegible]	[illegible]
95¼	Portobello 689, 720,			8 13	8 47	11 9		1 6				4 49	6 45	7 43				8 56					10 1		8 16
98	South Leith ....arr.			8 37	9 1	1228		1q51				5 8													
96¾	Piershill			8 17									6 49												8 21
97¾	Abbeyhill ..[695, 706			8 22									6 53											8 5	8 26
98¼	Edinbro' 702, 696, arr	6 45		8 26	8 55	1117	12 6	1 14		3 55		4 57	6 58	7 51	6 5		8 35	9 4			1025	6 45	10 9	8 10	8 30
145¼	702 Glasgow † ... arr.	8 50			1010	1 35	2 10	3 24		6 15		7 36	9 55	1025	7 50		1025					1043	7 48	9 55	
157¾	Dundee § 696 "	9 8			1118	g	3 37	3 37		6 15		8 10	10 3	1051	8 10		1051					9 15	8 19		
228¼	Aberdeen 696 "	1110			1 36		6 0	6 0		8 40		10 5		1250	10 5		1250					1120			
146	Perth ‡ 694 "	8 55		11 2	1131		3 35	3r35		6 21		7 52	9 45	1036	7 52		1036					8 40	7 20		
290	Inverness ‡ 775 "	1 50			4 20		8 40	8 40									5b10					1 30			

Column notes (printed vertically): Sleeping Car, St. Pancras to Edinbro' (first weekday column and first Sunday column). Via Peebles. Corridor Luncheon and Dining Car Express (1&3 class), London (St. Pancras) to Edinburgh. † Via Forth Bridge. § Via Forth and Tay Bridge. * Lime Street. † Queen Street. Corridor Luncheon and Dining Car Express (1&3 class), St. Pancras to Edinburgh. Corridor Luncheon and Dining Car Express (1&3 class), St. Pancras to Carlisle.

a Leaves at 12 55 on Monday mornings. b Does not arrive on Sunday mornings. e Passengers not guaranteed to be conveyed from this station. f Stops on Mondays when required t set down from South of Hawick. g Saturday night. h Saturdays only. i Leaves Leeds at 1 48 and Bradford at 1 30 on Monday mornings. k Arrives at 3 10 aft. on Saturdays. m Stops when required to set down from South of Carlisle. o Stops to set down, and to take up for Edinbro' and beyond, and to take up Passengers arriving at Hawick by the 4 15 aft. from Newcastle for Galashiels. q Arrives 5 minutes earlier on Saturdays. r Arrives at 3 45 aft. on Saturdays. v Via Leeds.

December 1902

July 1924

CARLISLE, RICCARTON JUNCTION, HAWICK, GALASHIELS, and EDINBURGH.—L. & N. E.

Miles from Carlisle	Down.	Week Days. aft	mrn	mrn	ngt	mrn	mrn	aft	aft	mrn	aft	mrn	aft	mrn	aft	aft	mrn	aft	mrn	aft	aft	aft	aft	aft	Sundays. aft
	616 London (St. Pancras) dep	9 15			9 30					4 25				9 0			9 50		11 45		1215	1215			9x15
	328 " (Euston) .... "	9n20			11 45							5 0					10 0		10 40		1 30	1 30		1 30	9x20
	328 Manchester (Exch.) "	11K0			1 10							9b15							1A30		4 15	4 15		5 0	
	328 " (Vic.). "									9 40		9 40		12 30					1 40		4 25	4 25		4 25	
	616 " (Vic.) * "									9 20							11B25				2 50	2 50			
	328 Liverpool (LimeSt.) "	10y40			12 45							9 50							1 50		3 30	3 30		4 20	
	328 " (Exch.).. "				1 50					9 47		9 47		12 40					1 45		4 5	4 5		5 8	
	616 " (Exch.) * "									9 15							11 10				2 53	2 53			
	616 Leeds (Wellington) "	1V47			2 10					1018				1 22			1 48		4 3		4 12	4 12			1 47
	616 Bradford ¶ ...... "	1 42								9 48				12 58					2Z58		3 20	3 20		3 37	1 42
		mrn	mrn	mrn	mrn	mrn	mrn	aft	aft	aft	aft	aft	aft	aft	aft	aft	aft	aft	aft	aft	aft	aft	aft	aft	mrn
—	Carlisle ....dep.	4 28			8 0	9 0				1 5		2 51		3 46			4 43		6 28		7 58	8 10		9 10	4 28
4¼	Harker				8 9							3 1					4 54				8 9	8 21			
6¾	Lyneside				8 14							3 6					4 59								
9¼	Longtown				8 23					1 21		3 13					5 10				8 23	8 35		9 25	
11¾	Scotch Dyke				8 29							3 19					5 15				8 28	8 40			
14¼	Riddings 905				8 36					1 29		3 24					5 19		a		8 32	8 44		9 33	
16¾	Penton				8 44							3 32												9 39	
21¼	Kershope Foot				8 54							3 42												9 49	
24¼	Newcastleton				9 1	b				1 46		3 50							7 1					9 57	
28¾	Steele Road				9 12							4 2												10 9	
32¼	Riccarton Junction 915				9 24				1 38			4 13						6 53						1021	
	Shankend				9 36				1 50			4 26												1034	
38¼	Stobs				9 42				1 57			4 33						7 10						1041	
41½	Hawick arr.	5 36			9 49	10 8			2 4	2 24		4 41		4 53				7 17	7 39					1049	5 36
45¼	Hawick dep.	5 42	6 48	8 2	9 53	1012				2 28	2 35			4 56	5 5			7s22	7 43						5 42
49¾	Hassendean **		6 57		10 2						2 45				5 14			7s31							
53¼	Belses		7 6		10 9						2 53				5 22			7s39							
57¾	St. Boswells 884, 902 arr.	5 59	7 14	8 20	10 17	1029				2 45	3 2				5 31			7s46	8 0						d
	St. Boswells 884, 902 dep.	6 1	7 15	8 24	10 20	1034				2 50	3 5		5 2		5 34			7s48	8 1						
61	Melrose		7 23	8 32	10 28	1041				2 57	3 13		5 8		5 41			7s56	8 8						
64¾	Galashiels 883, 906.. arr.	6 12	7 30	8 39	10 35	1047				3 3	3 20		5 14	5 21	5 48			8s3	8 14						6 12
	Galashiels 883, 906.. dep.	6 17	7 32	8 41		1050	1057			3 6	3 23			5 22	5 50				8 16	8 20					6 17
68¼	Bowland		7 41				11 7				3 33				5 59					8 29					
71¼	Stow		7 50	8 55			1115				3 41				6 7					8 37					
75¾	Fountainhall 915		8 0	9 4			1125				3 51				6 16					8 46					
79	Heriot		8 9				1134				4 0				6 25										
82¼	Tynehead ‖		8 16				1141				4 8				6 32										
85¼	Fushiebridge		8 23				1148				4 15				6 38										
86¾	Gorebridge		8 26	9 22			1151	2 3			4 18				6 41	6 48				9 4			10 0		
89¼	Newtongrange		8 31				1156	2 8			4 23					6 52				9 9			10 6		
90¼	Eskbank 903, 906		8 35	9 29			12 0	2 12			4 27				6 48	7 2				9 13			1011		
92	Millerhill, for Edmondstone							2 17			4 32					7 7				9 17			1016		
95¼	Portobello 882, 890, 902		8 44				12 9	2 23			4 39					7 13				9 23			1022		
96¼	Piershill [904																								
97¼	Abbeyhill [914																								
98¼	Edinburgh †† 886, 892, arr.	7 5	8 50	9 41		1138	1215	2 29		3 54	4 45			6 10	7 0	7 19			9 4	9 29			1028		7 5
145½	896 Glasgow (Q.S.) † 898 ar.	8 55	10 10	1115		2 5	2 5			5 5	6 15			7 30	9 46	9 46			10U40	1145					9 35
157½	886 Dundee (T.B.) ‡ .... "	9 18	11 22	1155		3 27	3 27			6 22	8 8			8 8	10 6	10 6									9 10
228½	886 Aberdeen ‡ .... "	11 19		1 46		5 25	5 25			8 40	10 5			10 5											1111
146	890 Perth (General) § . "	8 56	11 36	1136		2 35	2 35			6 19	7 53			7 53	1058	1058			10 58						9 5
264	890 Inverness § ...... "	2 45	3 50	3 50		7 50	7 50								6a0	6a0			6a0						

Column notes (printed vertically): Through Express, London (St. Pancras) to Edinburgh. Sleeping Car, London (St. Pancras) to Edinburgh. Through Carriage Bristol to Edinburgh (except on Saturdays), see page 562. Edinburgh, Dundee (Tay Bridge), and Aberdeen. Leaves Newcastle at 10 50 mrn., see pages 844 and 915. Leaves Kelso at 4 29 aft. see page 902. Restaurant Car Express, London (St. Pancras) to Edinburgh, Dundee, and Aberdeen. Through Train to Langholm, see page 905. Leaves Newcastle at 4 27 aft. see pages 844 and 915. Restaurant Car Express, London (St. Pancras) to Edinburgh. Saturdays only. Through Train to Langholm, see page 905. Except Saturdays. Through Train to Langholm, see page 905. Saturdays only. Saturdays only. Saturdays only. (Sundays:) Through Express, London (St. Pancras) to Edinburgh, Dundee (Tay Bridge), and Aberdeen. Sleeping Car, London (St. Pancras) to Edinburgh.

a Does not arrive on Sunday mornings. a Stops when required to take up, on notice being given to the Station Master. A Leaves at 1 25 aft. on Saturdays.
b Leaves at 9 10 mrn. on Saturdays. b Stops at Newcastleton on Stock Sale days. B Leaves at 12 20 aft. on Saturdays.
d Stops at St. Boswells at 5 59 mrn. when required to set down from South of Carlisle. K Leaves Manchester (Exchange at 11 20 aft. on Sundays.
n Leaves London (Euston) at 7 45 aft. on Sundays. s Saturdays only. U Low Level. V Leaves Leeds at 1 52 mrn. on Mondays. x Saturday night times.
y Leaves at 9 aft. on Sundays. Z Via Leeds. * Via Hellifield. † High Level. ‡ Via Forth and Tay Bridges. § Via Forth Bridge.
‖ Station for Pathhead Village (3½ miles). ¶ Forster Square. ** Station for Minto (1¼ miles). †† Waverley.

Table 167 EDINBURGH, CARLISLE, and LONDON St. Pancras)

Week Days (part 1)

Miles from Edinburgh	Station	a.m	a.m	a.m	a.m	p.m	p.m S	a.m	a.m S	a.m	p.m S
217	INVERNESS A .... dep	..	..	..	..	..	..	..	..	..	..
185	INVERNESS B .... "	..	..	..	..	11U20	..	..	..	..	..
185	PERTH .... "	..	..	..	..	8a13	..	9 10	9 10	9 10	..
184	ABERDEEN .... "	..	..	..	..	5 55	..	..	..	..	..
184	DUNDEE (TayBridge) "	..	..	..	..	7 51	..	8 40	9 40	9 40	..
201	GLASGOW (Q'nSt.) 204 "	..	..	..	6 30	8 30	..	10 0	1120	1120	..
		a.m	a.m	a.m	a.m	a.m	p.m	non	p.m	p.m	p.m
—	**Edinburgh** (Waverley) . dep		..	6 20	8 24	10 10	..	12 0	1257	1 3	..
1	Abbeyhill	TC Hawick to Newcastle arr. 9 11 a.m. (Tables 163 and 154)	..	6 23	..	RC and TC Edinburgh (W.) to London (St.P.)	..		..	..	..
1¾	Piershill		..	6 27	..		..		..	1 9	..
3	Portobello		..	6 31	8 30		..		..	1 12	
6½	Millerhill		..	6 38	8 37		..		..	1 19	Saturdays only
8	Eskbank		..	6 44	8 43		..	Buffet Car	1 11	1 24	
9¾	Newtongrange		..	6 49	8 49		..		1 16	1 29	
12	Gorebridge		..	6 57	8 57		..		1 23	1 35	
16	Tynehead		..	7 7	9 11		..		1 35	..	
19	Heriot		..	7 16	9 21		..		1 43	..	
22½	Fountainhall		..	7 22	9 28		..		1 50	..	
26¾	Stow		..	7 31	9 35		..		1 57	..	
29¾	Bowland		..	7 37	9 42				2 4	..	
33½	**Galashiels** ...... arr		..	7 44	9 49	11 1	Saturdays only	1251	2 11	..	..
	dep		..	7 50	9 51	11 4		1253	2 18	..	3 5
37½	Melrose		..	7 58	9 58	11 11		1 0	2 25	..	3 12
40½	St. Boswells ...... arr		..	8 5	10 5	11 17		1 6	2 32	..	3 19
	dep		..	8 9	10 7	11 21		1 8	2 35	..	..
45½	Belses D		..	8 21	1016	..		..	2 46	..	..
48½	Hassendean		..	8 29	1023	..		..	2 52	..	..
52¾	**Hawick** .... arr		..	8 36	1030	11 36		1 23	3 1	..	..
	dep	6 15	..	8 41	..	11 42	1230	1 29		..	..
56¾	Stobs	6 25	..	8 51	..	..	1239	..	Saturdays only	..	..
59¾	Shankend	Cc	..	8 59	..	..	1247	..		..	..
65¾	Riccarton Junction	6 45	7 7	9 17	..	..	1 0	..		..	..
69¾	Steele Road	..	..	9 23	..	..	1 6	..		..	..
74	Newcastleton	..	7 19	9 32	..	..	1 13	..		..	..
77	Kershope Foot	..	7 25	9 38	..	..	1 19	..		..	..
81½	Penton	..	7 34	9 47	..	..	1 26	..		..	..
84½	Riddings	..	7 41	9 54	..	..	1 32	..		..	..
86¼	Scotch Dyke	..	7 47	9 59	..	..	1 37	..		..	..
88¼	Longtown	..	7 53	10 5	..	..	1 43	..		..	..
98¼	Carlisle .... arr	..	8 10	10 22	..	12 49	1 58	2 35		..	..
203	BRADFORD (ForsterSq) arr	..	..	..	..	3 57	..	8 46	..	..	..
211	LEEDS (City) ...... "	..	..	2 31	..	3 32	..	..	..	..	..
234½	LIVERPOOL (Exchange) "	..	12F42	..	..	4KF20	..	..	..	..	..
223¾	MANCHESTER (Vic.) ... "	..	12F31	..	..	4KF20	..	..	..	..	..
250½	SHEFFIELD .... "	..	..	3 36	..	4 40	..	..	..	..	..
291	NOTTINGHAM .... "	..	..	5 13	..	5 55	..	..	..	..	..
309¾	LEICESTER .... "	..	..	5 15	..	7 13	..	..	..	..	..
327¾	BIRMINGHAM (NewSt.) "	..	..	5 59	..	7 25	..	..	..	..	..
416½	BRISTOL (Tem. Meads) "	..	..	8 17	..	12D15	..	..	..	..	..
408¾	**London** (St. Pancras) . "	..	..	7 30	..	9 10	..	..	..	..	..

Week Days (part 2) and **Sundays**

Miles from Edinburgh	Station	a.m	p.m	p.m	a.m	a.m	a.m	p.m SC	p.m	p.m S	Sun a.m	Sun p.m	Sun p.m SC	Sun p.m
217	INVERNESS A .... dep	..	..	..	7 40	7 40	7 40	12 45	1245	..	..	..	..	..
185	INVERNESS B .... "	8 40	..	..	11 0	11 0	11 0	3 45	3 45	..	..	..	3 10	3 10
185	PERTH .... "	12p25	..	..	3p27	3p27	3p27	7 55	7 55	..	..	..	8 0	8 0
184	ABERDEEN .... "	9a30	..	..	1240	1240	1240	5 20	5 20	..	..	3 37	3 37	3 37
184	DUNDEE (TayBridge) "	11 27	..	1228	2 43	2 50	2 50	7 16	7 16	..	8 30	5 33	6 5	6 5
201	GLASGOW (Q'nSt.) 204 "	1p 0	..	2 25	2 25	4 0	5 0	8 0	8 0	..	9 35	6 0	8 0	8 0
		p.m	p.m	p.m	p.m	p.m	p.m	p.m	p.m	p.m	a.m	p.m	p.m	p.m
—	**Edinburgh** (Waverley) . dep	2 35		4 10	5 20	5 53	7 2	9 55	1015	1035	11 20	8 20	9 55	1015
1	Abbeyhill	..	TC Hawick to Newcastle, arr. 8 2 p.m. (Tables 163 and 154)	..	..	..	7 5	TC Edinburgh (W.) to London (St. Pancras)	..	..	..	..	TC Edinburgh (W.) to London (St. Pancras)	..
1¾	Piershill	..		..	..	..	7 8		..	..	..	..		..
3	Portobello	..		4 16	5 26	..	7 12		..	1041	11 26	8 26		..
6½	Millerhill	..		4 23	..	..	7 19		..	1048	..	..		..
8	Eskbank	..		4 28	5 35	..	7 25		..	1054	11 36	8 36		..
9¾	Newtongrange	..		4 34	5 40	..	7 31		..	11 1	..	..		..
12	Gorebridge	..		4 42	5 46	..	7 38		..	11 7	..	..		..
16	Tynehead	..		4 55	..	..	7 49		..		..	..		..
19	Heriot	..		5 5	..	..	7 58		..	Saturdays only	..	..		..
22½	Fountainhall	..		5 11	..	6 33	8 4		..		..	..		..
26¾	Stow	3 20		5 18	..	6 40	8 12		..		..	..		..
29¾	Bowland	..		5 25	..	..	8S19		..		..	..		..
33½	**Galashiels** ...... arr	3 30		5 32	..	6 50	8 26	10 46	11 6		12 21	9 17	10 46	11 6
	dep	3 33		5 35	..	6 52	8 31	10 50	1114		12 22	9 19	10 50	1114
37½	Melrose	3 40		5 42	..	6 59	8 39	10 57	1123		12 28	9 27	10 57	1123
40½	St. Boswells ...... arr	3 46		5 49	..	7 5	8 46	..	1129		12 35	9 34	..	1129
	dep	3 51		5 56	..	7 8	8 49	..	1133		12 36	9 36	..	1133
45½	Belses D	..		6 7	..	..	8 58	..	..	..	..	9 45	..	..
48½	Hassendean	..		6 15	..	..	9 6	..	..	..	..	..	..	..
52¾	**Hawick** .... arr	4 7		6 22	..	7 23	9 13	11 16	1148	..	12 53	9 56	11 16	1148
	dep	4 13	4 30	..	..	7 28	9N20	11 21	1155	..	..	..	11 21	1155
56¾	Stobs	4 22	4 41	..	..	..	9N30	..	..	..	..	..	..	..
59¾	Shankend	4 31	4 49	..	..	..	9N38	..	..	..	..	..	..	..
65¾	Riccarton Junction	4 45	5 1	..	..	..	9N48	..	..	..	..	..	..	..
69¾	Steele Road	4 51	..	..	..	..	..	..	..	..	..	..	..	..
74	Newcastleton	5 0	..	..	..	8 9	..	..	..	..	..	..	..	..
77	Kershope Foot	5 7	..	..	..	..	..	..	..	..	..	..	..	..
81½	Penton	5 16	..	..	..	..	..	..	..	..	..	..	..	..
84½	Riddings	5 23	..	..	..	..	..	..	..	..	..	..	..	..
86¼	Scotch Dyke	5 29	..	..	..	..	..	..	..	..	..	..	..	..
88¼	Longtown	5 38	..	..	..	8 27	..	..	..	..	..	..	..	..
98¼	Carlisle .... arr	5 54	..	..	..	8 41	..	12a26	1 a 5	..	..	..	12a26	1 a 5
203	BRADFORD (ForsterSq) arr	10 6	..	..	..	..	..	4 21	5Y23	..	..	..	4 21	..
211	LEEDS (City) ...... "	9 39	..	..	..	2u34	..	3 2	4B35	..	..	..	3 2	..
234½	LIVERPOOL (Exchange) "	9F50	..	..	..	..	..	..	6R30	..	..	..	..	6P30
223¾	MANCHESTER (Vic.) ... "	10F15	..	..	..	..	..	..	6d10	..	..	..	..	6T10
250½	SHEFFIELD .... "	11 6	..	..	..	3u43	..	4 10	..	..	..	..	4 10	..
291	NOTTINGHAM .... "	1 45	..	..	..	..	..	5 28	..	..	..	..	5 28	..
309¾	LEICESTER .... "	1 51	..	..	..	5u29	..	7Z2	..	..	..	..	7 2	..
327¾	BIRMINGHAM (NewSt.) "	1‡40	..	..	..	..	..	7L50	..	..	..	..	7 50	..
416½	BRISTOL (Tem. Meads) "	4‡35	..	..	..	..	..	11L52	..	..	..	..	11 52	..
408¾	**London** (St. Pancras) . "	5c40	..	..	..	7u55	..	8L30	..	..	..	..	8 30	..

Y Sunday morns only. Via Leeds   Z Arr. 7 31 a.m. on Sundays   ‡ Arrive Birmingham (N.St.) 2 5 and Bristol (T.M.) 5 50 a.m. on Sundays

- A Via Aberdeen
- a a.m.
- B Via Dunkeld
- B Sunday morns only
- Cc Calls at 6 33 a.m. when required to take up on informing the Sta. Master at Stobs before 5 0 p.m. the day previous to travel
- c Arr. 5 20 a.m. on Sundays
- D Station for Ancrum and Lilliesleaf
- D Arr. 11 19 p.m on Saturdays.
- d Manchester (Ex.) via Preston, arr. 6 20 a.m. on Sundays
- E or E Except Sats.
- F Via Preston
- K Arr. Liverpool (Ex.) 4 28 and Manchester (Vic.) 4 30 p.m. Via Hellifield
- L Arr. St. Pancras 8 20 a.m., Birmingham (N. St.) 8 24 a.m. and Bristol (T. M.) 1 0 p.m on Sundays
- N Mons., Weds., and Sats.
- P Lime St. Station via Preston
- p p.m.
- R Lime Street Sta. via Preston: arr. 6 40 a.m. on Sundays
- RC Restaurant Car
- S or S Saturdays only
- SC Limited Sleeping accommodation. Does not convey Sleeping Car Passengers from Edinburgh (Wav.) to London (St. Pan.)
- T Exchange Station, via Preston
- TC Through Carriages
- U Except Saturday and Sunday nights
- u Except Sunday morns

October 1947

May 1968

Carlisle to Edinburgh via Hawick

Weekdays (part 1)

Miles	Station		🛏	SX					B	D SO	SX	SO
—	LONDON EUSTON	d	22j15	..	..	..	..	..	..	..	..	..
—	LONDON ST. PANCRAS	d	21j15	..	..	..	..	..	..	..	..	..
—	CARLISLE	d	04 44	..	..	..	09 20	..	..	..	13 00	13 00
9¼	LONGTOWN	d	..	..	..	..	09 37	..	..	..	13 16	13 16
16¾	PENTON	d	..	..	..	..	09 49	..	..	..	..	13 28
21½	KERSHOPE FOOT	d	..	..	..	..	09 57	..	..	..	13 34	13 36
24½	NEWCASTLETON	d	05 17	..	..	..	10 03	..	..	..	13 40	13 42
28¾	STEELE ROAD	d	..	..	..	..	10 12	..	..	..	13 49	13 51
32¼	RICCARTON JUNCTION	d	..	..	..	..	10 20	..	..	..	13 57	13 59
38¼	SHANKEND	d	..	..	..	..	10 32	..	..	..	14 08	14 10
41¼	STOBS	d	..	..	..	..	10 39	..	..	..	14 15	14 17
45¼	HAWICK	a	05 49	..	..	..	10 46	..	..	..	14 22	14 24
		d	05 54	..	06 58	08 15	10 50	..	12 05	12 05	14 28	14 30
49¾	HASSENDEAN	d	..	..	..	08 22	10 57	..	12 13	12 13	..	..
53	BELSES	d	..	..	..	08 28	11 03	..	12 20	12 20	..	..
57¾	ST. BOSWELLS	a	06 08	..	07 12	08 34	11 09	..	12 27	12 27	14 42	14 44
		d	06 12	..	07 13	08 35	11 11	..	12 28	12 28	14 43	14 46
61	MELROSE	d	06 18	..	07 19	08 41	11 17	..	12 34	12 34	14 49	14 52
61¾	GALASHIELS	a	06 24	..	07 25	08 47	11 23	..	12 40	12 40	14 55	14 58
		d	06 29	..	07 26	08 48	11 27	..	12 41	12 41	15 00	15 00
71¼	STOW	d	..	..	07 38	09 00	..	..	12 55	12 55	..	..
75¾	FOUNTAINHALL	d	..	..	07 45	09 06	..	..	13 03	13 03	..	..
79¼	HERIOT	d	..	..	07 52	09 13	..	..	13 11	13 11	..	..
82¼	TYNEHEAD	d	..	..	07h58	..	..	..	..	..	..	..
86¼	GOREBRIDGE	d	..	..	08g04	..	..	..	13 22	13 22	..	..
88¼	NEWTONGRANGE	d	..	..	08g09	..	..	..	13 27	13 27	..	..
90¼	ESKBANK & DALKEITH	d	..	08 05	08g13	09 29	..	..	13 31	13 31	..	..
98¼	EDINBURGH	a	07 12	08 17	08g26	09 42	12 13	..	13 46	13 46	15 46	15 46
	18 PERTH	a	09 05	..	10 52	12 05	14 24	..	16 08	16 08	17 35	17 35
	18 ABERDEEN	a	10 45	..	..	13f20	16 20	..	17 40	17 40	19 40	19 40
	15 GLASGOW QUEEN STREET	a	08 37	..	09 56	10f56	13 44	..	14 56	14 56	16 56	16 56

Weekdays (part 2) and **Suns.**

Miles	Station		H SO		B ✕	D SO	A ✕ 🛏	E SO	SX			Suns. 🛏	Suns.	Suns.
—	LONDON EUSTON	d	..	..	10 05	..	10 05	..	12 05	14 05	..	22e15	..	..
—	LONDON ST. PANCRAS	d	..	..	09 05	..	09 55	..	..	..	..	21e15	..	..
—	CARLISLE	d	13 25	..	15 47	..	17 00	..	18 13	19 44	..	04 46	..	..
9¼	LONGTOWN	d		..		..		..	18 32	20 00	..	..	..	..
16¾	PENTON	d		..		..		..	18 44	..	..	..	..	..
21½	KERSHOPE FOOT	d		..		..		..	18 52	..	..	..	..	..
24½	NEWCASTLETON	d		..	16 22	..	17 33	..	18 58	20 21	..	..	..	..
28¾	STEELE ROAD	d		..		..		..	..	..	..	..	..	..
32¼	RICCARTON JUNCTION	d		..		..		..	19 16	20 35	..	..	..	..
38¼	SHANKEND	d		..		..		..	19 27	..	..	..	..	..
41¼	STOBS	d		..		..		..	19 33	..	..	..	..	..
45¼	HAWICK	a	14 40	..	16 54	..	18 03	..	19 40	20 55	..	05 50	..	..
		d	14 45	..	17 00	17 04	18 07	18 04	..	20 58	..	05 56	08 30	18 16
49¾	HASSENDEAN	d		..					..	..	..	..	..	..
53	BELSES	d		..					..	21e09	..	..	..	..
57¾	ST. BOSWELLS	a	15 00	..	17 14	17 20	18 21	18 20	..	21y12	..	06 10	08 46	18 32
		d	15 02	..	17 18	17 21	18 24	18 21	..	21y14	..	06 14	08 47	18 33
61	MELROSE	d	15 09	..	17 24	17 27	18 30	18 27	..	21y20	..	06 20	08 53	18 39
61¾	GALASHIELS	a	15 15		17 30	17 33	18 36	18 33	..	21y26	..	06 26	08 59	18 45
		d	15 17	..	17 36	17 34	18 41	18 34	..	21z29	..	06 31	09 00	18 46
71¼	STOW	d		..					..	..	..	..	..	..
75¾	FOUNTAINHALL	d		..					..	..	..	..	..	..
79¼	HERIOT	d		..	The Waverley				..	..	..	..	..	..
82¼	TYNEHEAD	d		..					..	..	..	..	..	..
86¼	GOREBRIDGE	d		..					..	..	..	..	..	..
88¼	NEWTONGRANGE	d		..					..	..	..	..	..	..
90¼	ESKBANK & DALKEITH	d		18 03					..	..	..	..	..	..
98¼	EDINBURGH	a	16 02	18 15	18 19	18 23	19 23	19 23	..	22z16	..	07 14	09 49	19 35
	18 PERTH	a	17 35	20 35	20 35	20 35	22 36	22 36	..	00 35	..	09 25	..	21 25
	18 ABERDEEN	a	19 40	21 50	21 50	21 50	23 20	23 20	..	03n20	..	10 42	..	..
	15 GLASGOW QUEEN STREET	a	17 41	19 41	19 41	19 56	20 41	20 56	..	23 41	..	08 40	11 40	21 40

Heavy figures denote through carriages
Light figures denote connecting services

- A Until 8 June and from 30 September. ✕ and 🛏 London to Carlisle
- B 10 June to 28 September
- C Until 8 June and from 30 September ✕ and 🛏 Carlisle to London
- D Until 8 June and from 5 October
- E 15 June to 28 September
- G 29 June to 10 August. Through carriages Dundee dep. 09 15 to Blackpool North
- H 6 July to 17 August. Through carriages Blackpool North dep. 10 44 to Dundee
- b On Sundays arr. 06 00
- c On Sundays arr. 08 30
- e Saturdays only
- f On Saturdays from 29 June to 10 August arr. 13 12
- g 2 minutes earlier on Saturdays.
- h Except Saturdays
- j Sundays to Fridays
- k Change at Carlisle and Preston
- n Except Sundays
- r From 17 June to 21 October arr. 06 25
- v Saturdays excepted departs 19 33
- y 3 minutes later on Saturdays
- z 2 minutes later on Saturdays

GALASHIELS

III. Galashiels was first mentioned in 1124 although there were settlements dating back to the iron age nearby. The town's long association with the Textile trade began in 1585 and by 1825 there were 35 mills in operation. This led to rapid expansion and in 1891 the population was 18,000. As the number of mills reduced then so did the population and had reduced to 12,935 in 1960 and to 12,367 in 2011. The town joined the railway network on 20th February 1849 for the first time until closure to passengers on 6th January 1969 and complete abandonment in 1971. 1932 map at 25" to 1 mile.

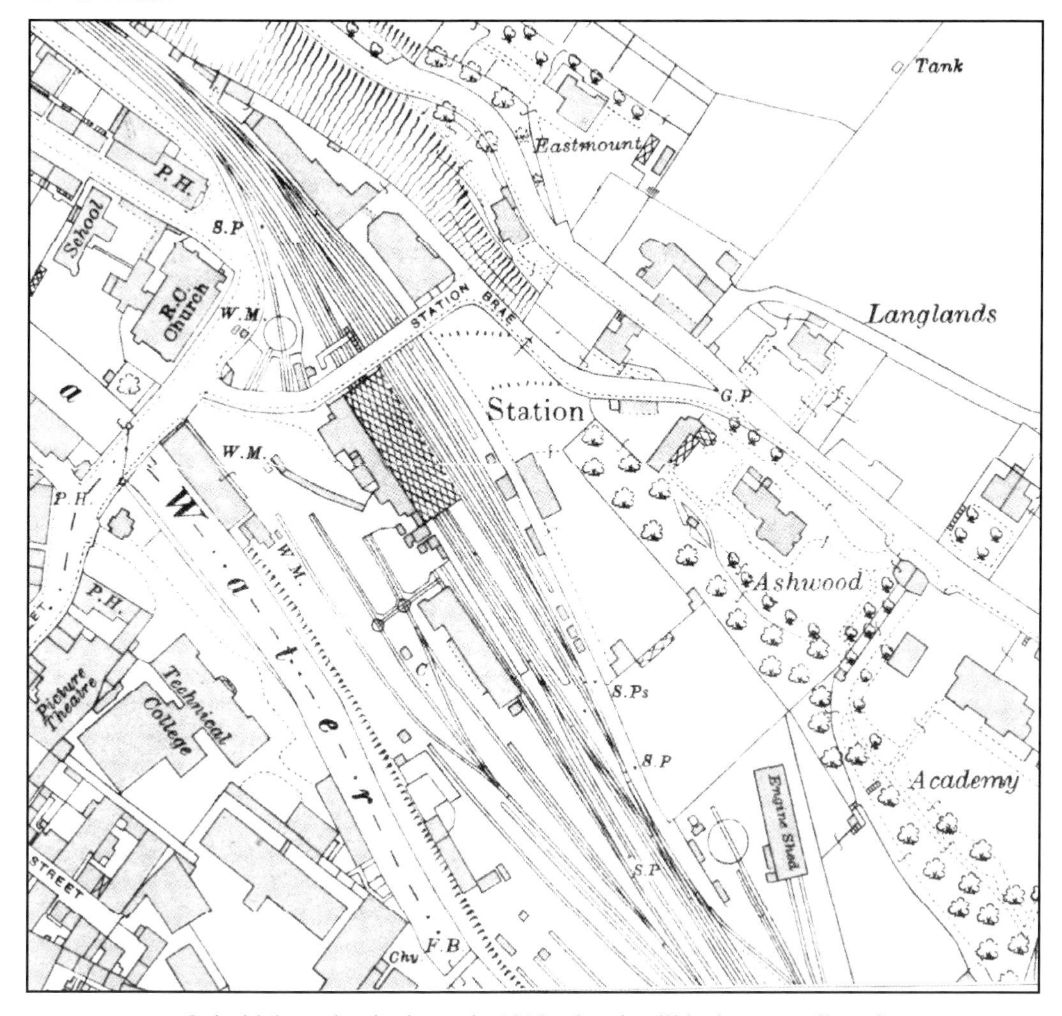

Galashiels station is shown in 1932 when it still had an overall roof.

Further pictures of Galashiels station and engine shed can be found in our *Hawick to Galashiels* album.

1. NBR Atlantic class H no.873 *Saint Mungo* passes the Abbotsford Hotel in Ladhope Vale. The new station for the reinstated railway will be located behind the hotel building which still fulfils its original purpose. (Old Gala Club)

2. Steam from the safety valves was going where neither the driver nor the photographer wanted it as D49/2 class 4-4-0 no.266 *Forfarshire* leaves Galashiels with the 12.00 from Edinburgh to St. Pancras in the mid 1930s. Note the headboard and the Pullman dining car. A K2 class 2-6-0, possibly no.4689, is in the Galashiels shed roads. (A.G.Ellis/R.W.Lynn coll.)

3. We are looking south towards Melrose. The island platform is served by the footbridge with split steps giving access to it. Most facilities were on the Down platform including a John Menzies kiosk. (N. Forrest/Transport Treasury)

Further pictures of Galashiels station and loco shed can be found in our *Hawick to Galashiels* album.

4. This is an overall view of Galashiels shed on 10th July 1952 showing the coal loading sidings and ash pits. Class D34 4-4-0 no.62471 *Glen Falloch* was on shed. (N.E.Stead coll.)

KILNKNOWE JUNCTION

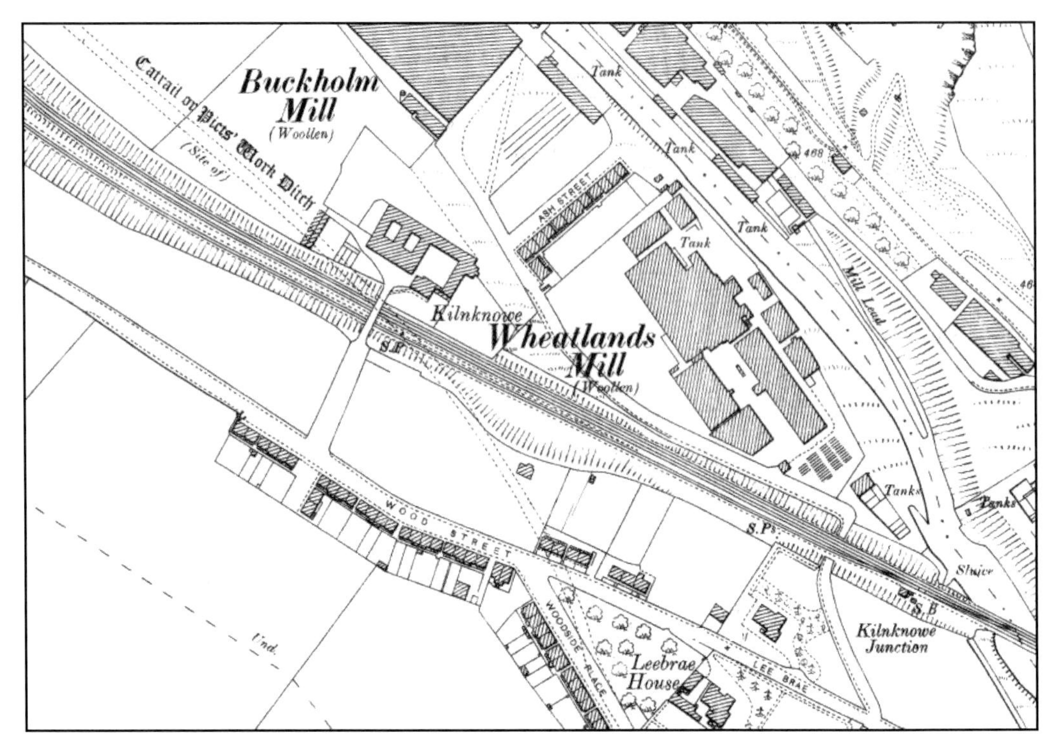

IV. Kilnknowe Junction located 1.1 miles north of Galashiels was where the line from Peebles (opened on 1st October 1864) joined the Waverley route. This provided an alternative through route between Galashiels and Edinburgh via Peebles. The line to Peebles closed on 3rd February 1962 and the tracks serving the third platform at Galashiels was removed soon after. 1898 map is at 15" to 1 mile.

5. A northbound local train heads for Edinburgh Waverley hauled by A3 Class no. 60095 *Flamingo* and passes Kilnknowe Junction in January 1950. The line on the right is the route to Peebles. (J.R.Smith/Colour Rail)

BOWLAND

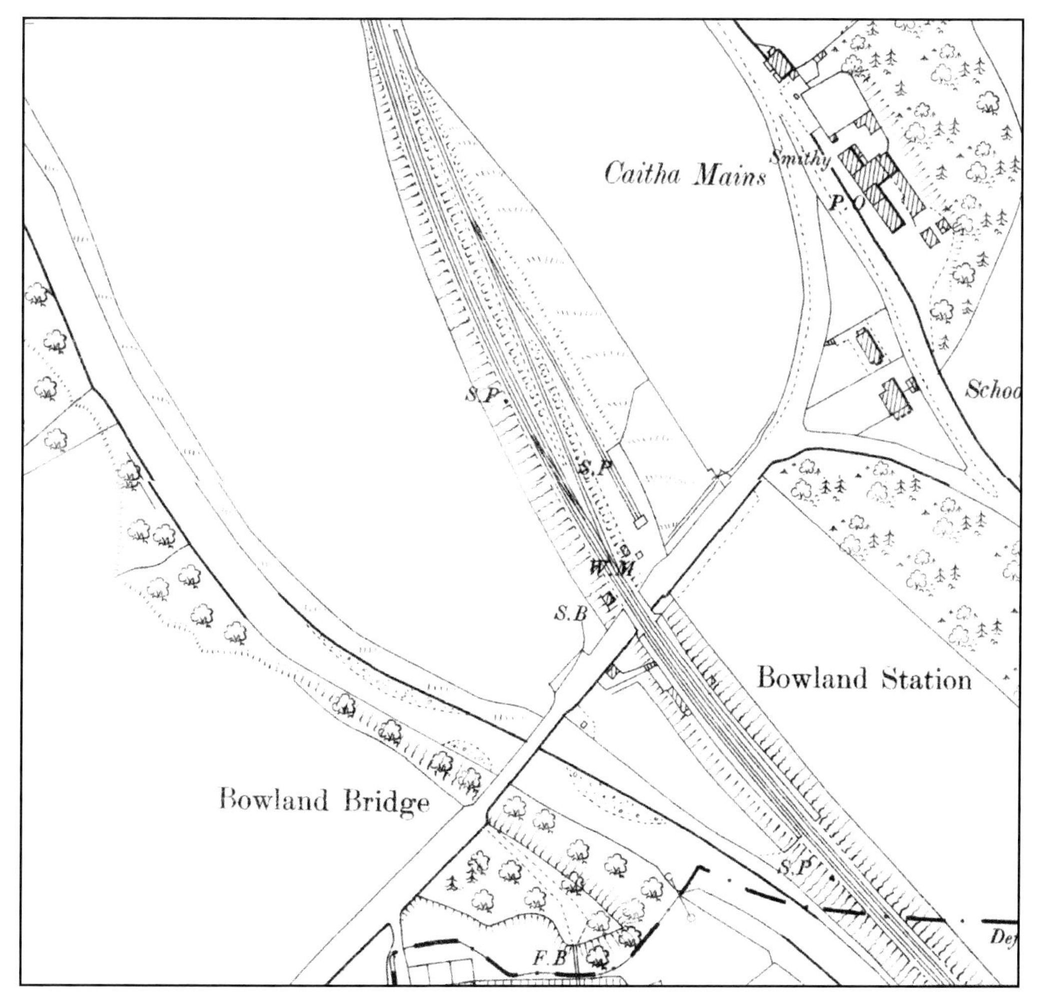

V. Bowland opened on 1st May 1848 and was for a short time the southern terminus of the line until completion of Torwoodlee Tunnel allowed entry to Galashiels. The station became Bowland Bridge in May 1849 before reverting to its original name in July 1862. The station closed to passengers on 7th December 1953 and to goods traffic on 23rd March 1964. Bowshank Tunnel was located to the north of the goods yard. 1898 map at 25" to 1 mile.

1746
British Railways (S1) For conditions see back | British Railways (S1) For conditions see back
THIRD CLASS | THIRD CLASS
SINGLE | SINGLE
Bowland | Bowland
Bowland To
GALASHIELS
Galashiels | Galashiels
-/10½ Z | -/10½ Z
1746

0025
EDINBURGH ZOOLOGICAL GARDENS
ADMIT ONE JUVENILE
To be given up at Turnstile
FOR CONDITIONS SEE BACK.
L.N.E.R. BOWLAND
0025

6. The main station building on the Down platform also served as the local post office. It was a small building reflecting its rural location. The station closed to passenger traffic on 7th December 1953.
(Lens Of Sutton Association /LOSA)

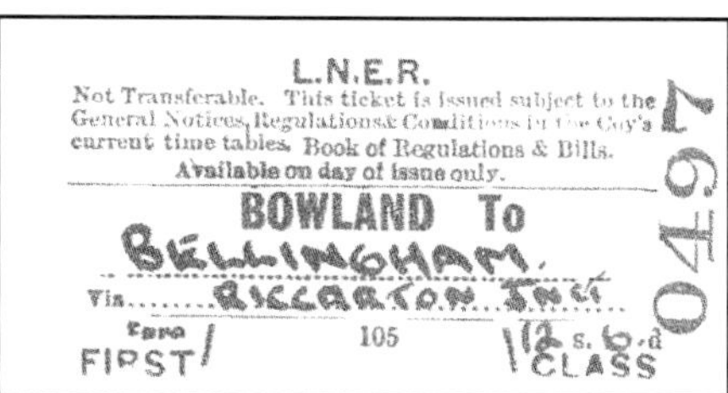

7. The Up platform had only a small waiting shelter on an otherwise exposed platform. The station served only a very small community and the adjacent Bowland House. (LOSA)

8. With a goods train heading north away from the station the trailing point on the Down line leads to the modest goods facilities which were at a lower level. (C.J.B.Sanderson /ARPT)

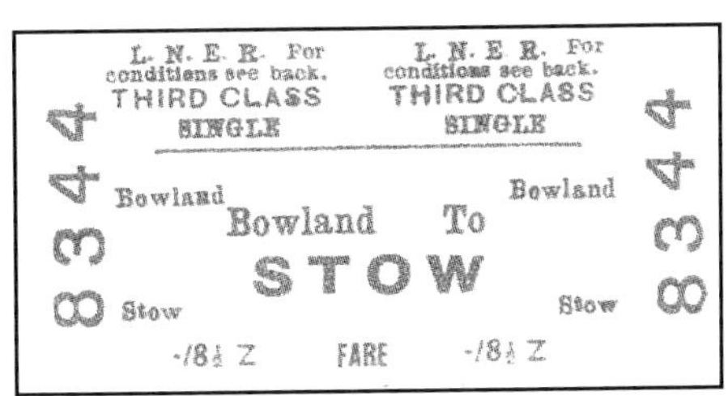

9. The southern portal of Bowshank Tunnel is seen here on 31st July 2012. Work was underway in readiness for reopening. (D.A.Lovett)

STOW

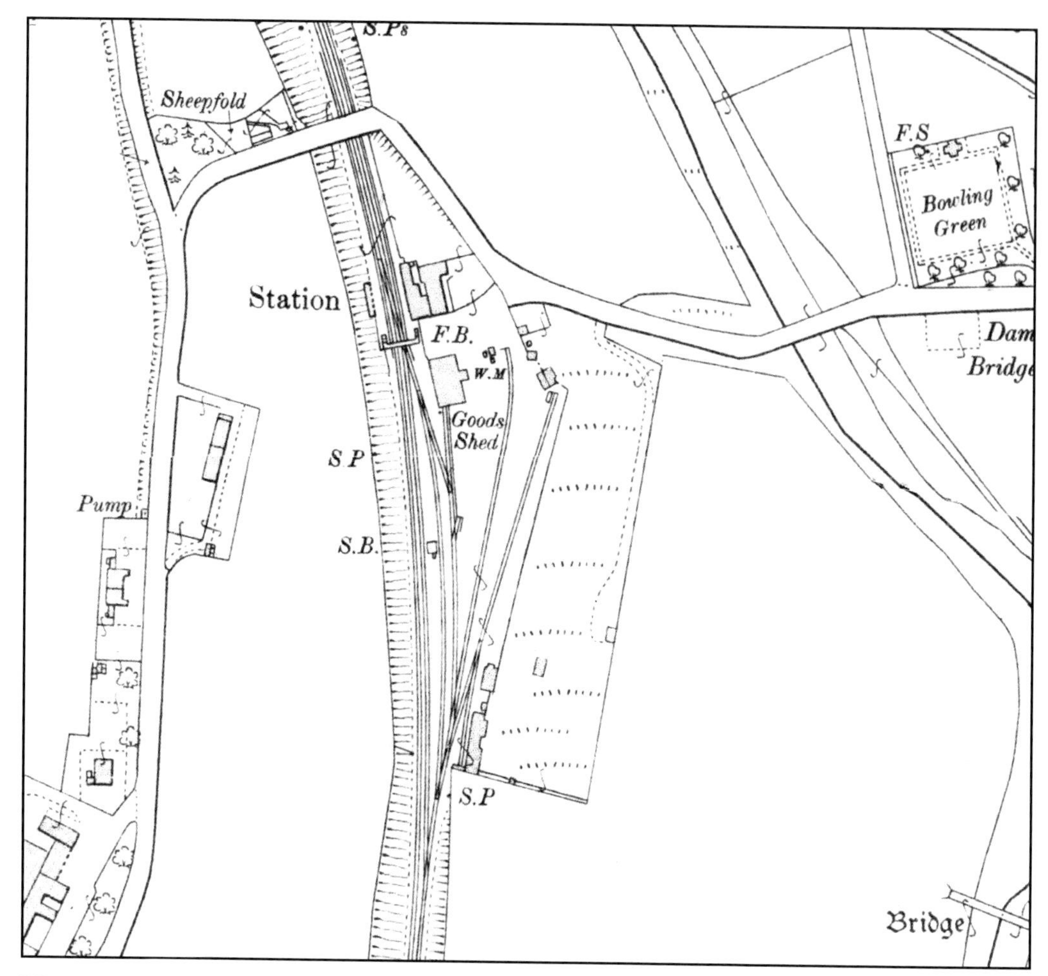

VI. Stow is located on the main A7 road from Galashiels to Edinburgh and in 1960 had a population of 462 (428 in 2011). The station opened on 1st November 1848. It closed for goods on 18th May 1964 and became an unstaffed halt on 27th March 1967. The station closed with the line on 6th January 1969. Stow was not included initially in the list of stations to be served by the reopened Waverley route but a local campaign saw it included. It was scheduled to reopen in 2015, the original station building still stands. 1907 map at 25" to 1 mile.

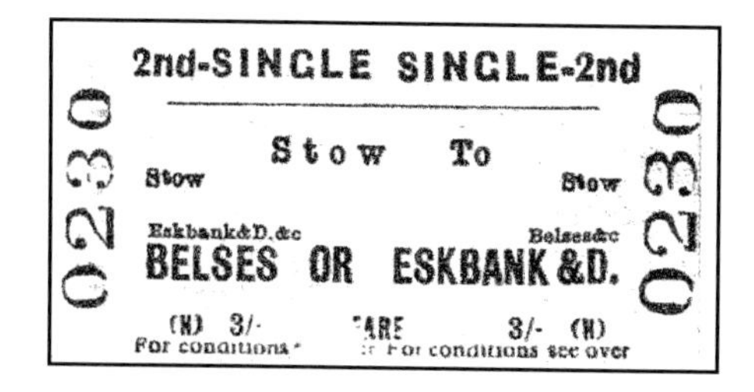

L. N. E. R.
FOR CONDITIONS SEE BACK. Available for three days, including day of issue.
0350
STOW to
FOUNTAINHALL
0350
Fare THIRD 101 8d.C CLASS
FOUNTAINHALL

10. An undated view from the early days of the 20th Century shows a south bound train hauled by 4-4-0 NBR Class M (D31) calling at the station. (J.Alsop coll.)

11. Looking north the platforms extend beyond the road bridge. The open area provides cover for the station handcart and no doubt passengers on occasions. (G.N.Turnbull/R.W.Lynn coll.)

12. Class V3 2-6-2T no.67669 was photographed in the station on a southbound local in 1955. This locomotive was the third Class V1 to be converted to V3 which was done in January 1943. (N.E.Stead coll.)

13. Stow station was located close to the centre of the village. Today the remaining buildings are surrounded by modern developments. The former goods yard is now home to the school. (H.D.Bowtell/R.W.Lynn coll.)

14. Until mid 2012 this view would have been blocked by a house constructed in front of the bridge. With work proceeding on the reopening the demolition contractors had removed it by the time it was photographed on 31st July 2012. The former down platform shelter is on the left and the main station building is on the up platform on the right. (D.A.Lovett)

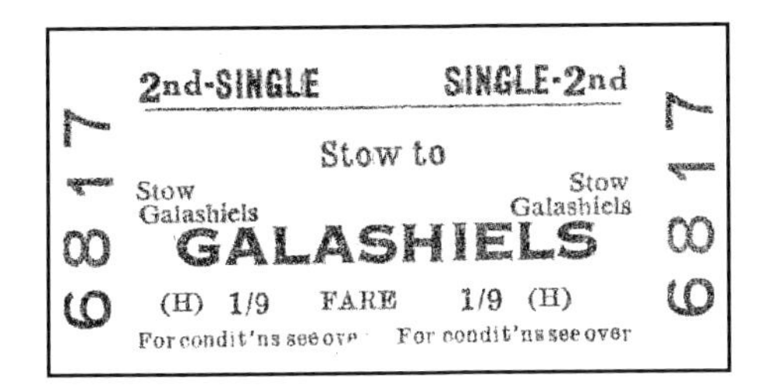

FOUNTAINHALL

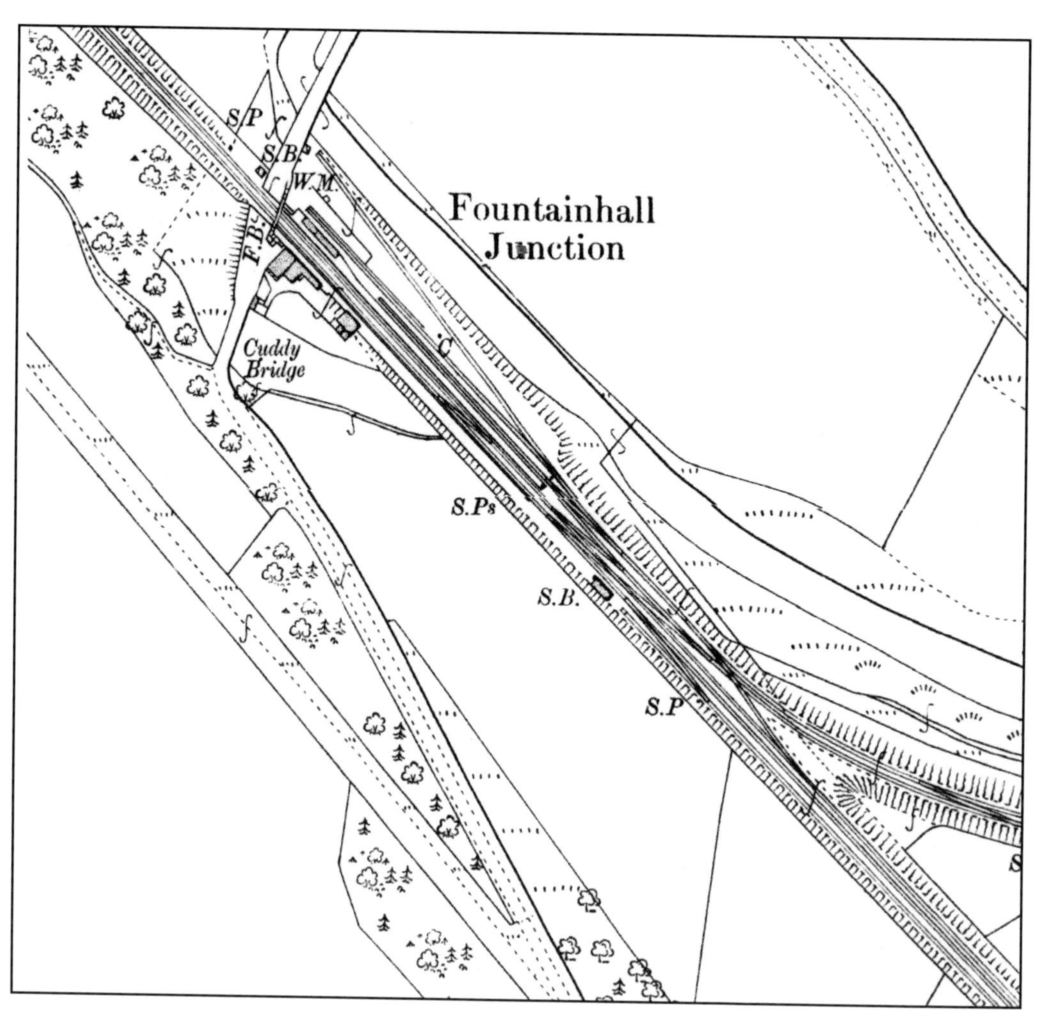

VII. Opened as Burn House on 1st August 1848, it was renamed Fountainhall in March 1849. The opening of the Lauder branch on 2nd July 1901 the station became Fountainhall Junction losing the suffix in April 1959. The station became an unstaffed halt on 27th March 1967 and closed with the line on 6th January 1969. After laying derelict for several years the station became a family home. During 2011 the station was once again boarded up pending the reinstatement of the line between Edinburgh and Tweedbank. There are no plans to reopen a station on this site. 1907 map at 25" to 1 mile.

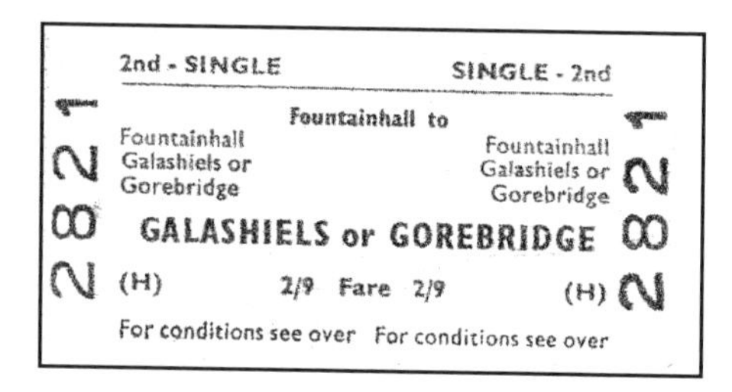

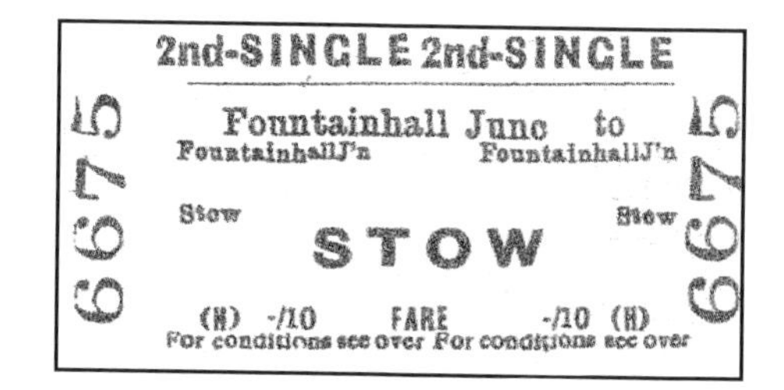

15. We are looking north with the down platform on the left. This picture dates from around 1906. (J.Alsop coll.)

16. A train for Lauder headed by North British Railway R Class 4-4-0T no. 33 waits in the bay platform around 1909. (J.Clapperton/Clapperton Trust.)

17. Now we are looking south with a van standing in the bay platform used by Lauder branch trains. (LOSA)

18. Stationmaster James Wilson Denholm centre is flanked by Porter Sandy Whitehead and an unknown clerk in this view dating from around 1930. (R.W.Lynn coll.)

19. The RCTS West Riding Tour over the Waverley Route on the last day of services on the line on 5th January 1969. Deltic no. D9007 *Pinza* operated from Leeds back to Leeds via Edinburgh and is seen here during the Fountainhall photo stop. It was the next to last train to traverse the line, the last being the sleeper from Edinburgh to London St. Pancras. (G.W.Morrison)

20. A visit in July 1976 saw the station derelict and the crossing gates had disappeared. The road can be seen at the end of the platform by the station building. The station building was later converted into a residential property. (D.A.Lovett)

OXTON

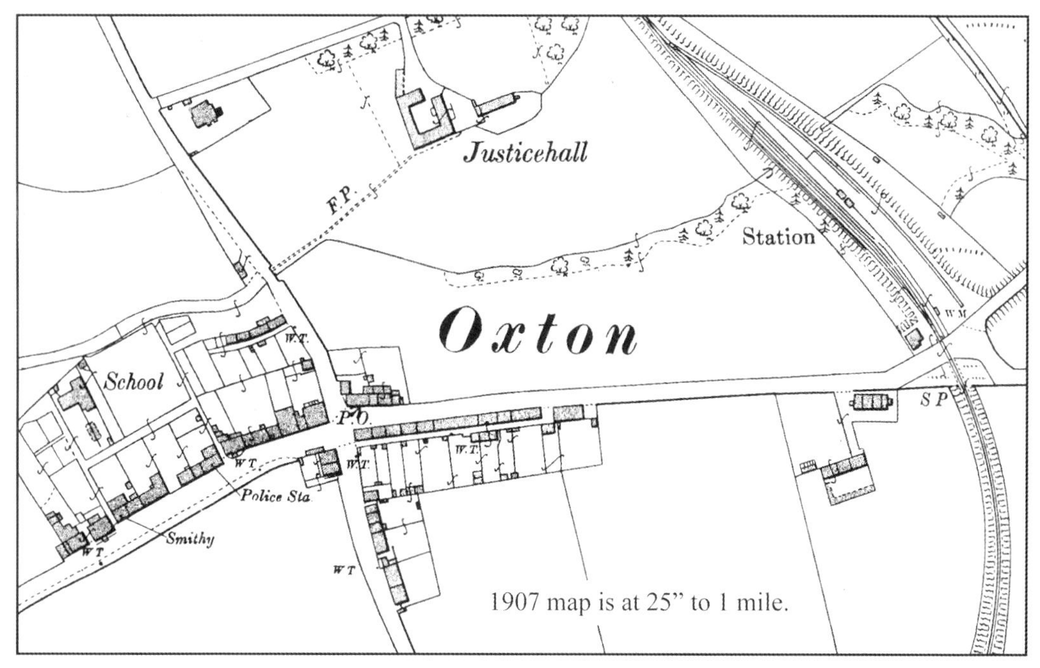

VIII. Oxton had a population of just 125 in 1960. The station had a passenger service for just 31 years opening on 2nd July 1901 and closing on 12th September 1932. Although the line remained open for freight it was closed by flooding between 12th August 1948 and 20th November 1950. The line finally closed to goods 1st October 1958 although it did see one final special train on 15th November of that year. The line was lifted and abandoned shortly afterwards. The crossing keepers house seen in picture 23 is now a private house. The distinctive Tower Hotel (seen below) in the centre of the village had recently been restored and reopened for business when it was photographed on 23 June 2013. (D.A.Lovett)

21. The first train to call at Oxton was this special on 28th June 1901 for the inspection by The Board of Trade. At that time some work was still outstanding such as the unfinished platform on the left. It was duly noted in the inspectors report. (J. Alsop coll.)

22. NBR Drummond R Class (D51) 0-4-4T no.52 poses with the station staff and dog for a commercial post card. The locomotive was originally called *Dirleton*. It was withdrawn in August 1933. (J. Alsop coll.)

23. The unconventional ungated level crossing is seen here. As a light railway there was no need to provide full crossing gates but there was a need to keep livestock off the line by installing cattle grids. (J.Alsop coll.)

24 Ivatt 2MT 2-6-0 no.46461 was photographed near Oxton with the branch goods. (C.J.B. Sanderson/ARPT)

LAUDER

IX. Like Oxton, Lauder was served by a passenger service for just 31 years opening on 2nd July 1901 and closing to passengers on 12th September 1932. After this Earlston on the line from St. Boswells to Berwick became the rail head for Lauder which was located on what is now the A68 trunk road. The line remained open for freight although it was closed by flooding between 12th August 1948 and 20th November 1950. The station lost its goods on 1st October 1958. Lauder had its own engine shed during the period of passenger operation. Latterly the line was served from Galashiels using J67 0-6-0 tank locomotives with tenders attached to carry additional water supplies. The single road shed can be seen in the middle of the track plan below. In 1939 a Ministry of Defence food buffer depot was opened at Lauder. This was rail served and provided much needed additional traffic on the line. Such depots stored valuable food stuffs for onward distribution should supplies be interrupted by bombing or invasion. 1907 map is at 25" to 1 mile.

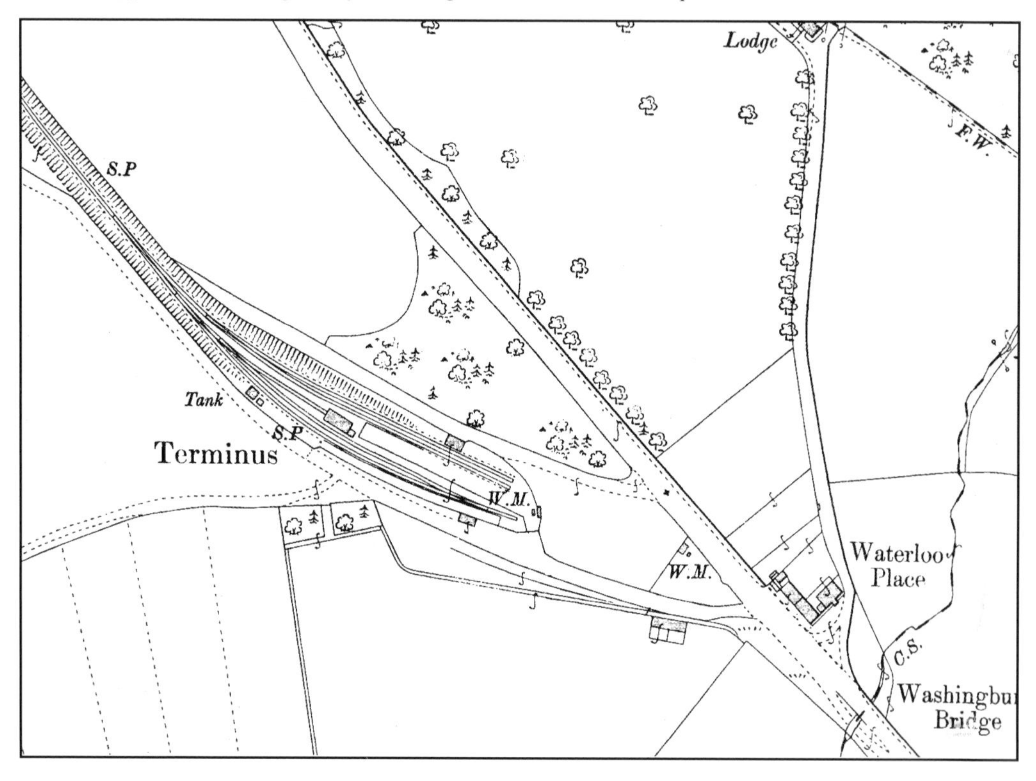

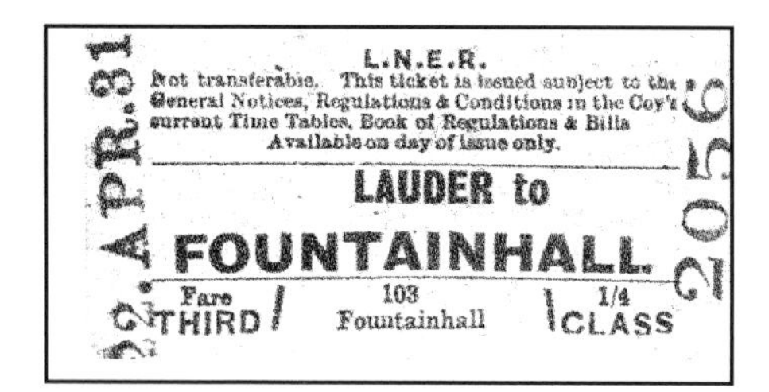

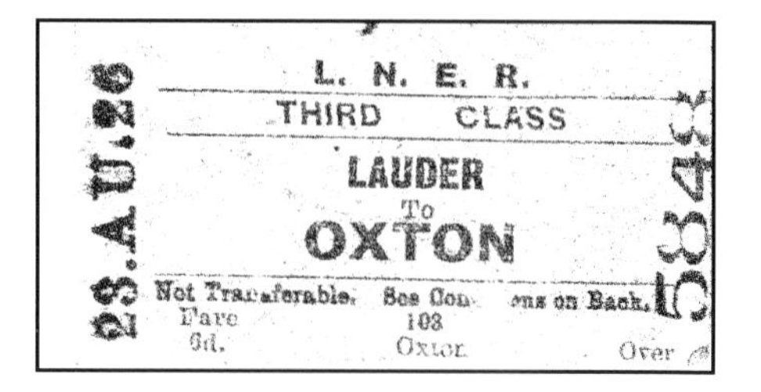

25. The digging of the first sod on the Lauder Light Railway took place at Horryburn on the outskirts of Lauder on the 3rd June 1899. The Countess of Lauderdale officiated. (J. Alsop coll.)

The working timetable of 1950 reflects the line when it was operated for freight only and after it had reopened following a two year closure as a result of flooding in 1948.

LAUDER LIGHT RAILWAY

UP TRAINS — WEEKDAYS

Distance from Fountainhall	No.	538‡	562		
	Description				
	Class	D	D		
M. C.		Q TO am	SX am		
	Fountainhall ....(T) ..	7 35	10F35	.....	.....
2 11	*Middleton Siding*	..	..	..	..
4 53	*Hortside Siding*	.....	.....	.....	.....
6 38	*Oxton* .. ..(T) ..	..	11 25	..	..
10 33	*Lauder*	8 15	11 35	.....	.....

No. 562—F Leaves Galashiels 9.45 a.m. Worked by Galashiels No. 1 Pilot Engine and Guard.

DOWN TRAINS — WEEKDAYS

Distance from Lauder	No.	517	533		
	Description	Live St'k			
	Class	D	D		
M. C.		Q TO am	SX PM		
	Lauder	8 40	12 5	.....	.....
3 75	*Oxton* .. .. (T)..	9 0	12 25	..	..
10 33	Fountainhall ...... (T)..	9F30	12F50	.....	.....

Nos. 517 and 533—F Arrive Galashiels 10.40 a.m. and 1.30 p.m. respectively.

26. NBR Drummond class R 4-4-0T (LNER D51) no.10406 departs for Lauder with a train from Fountainhall. Its NBR original number was 111 and it was named *Clackmannan*. It lasted until April 1933. (R.W.Lynn coll.)

27. The modest station facilities are extravagant by many light railway standards. (J.Clapperton/Clapperton Trust)

28. This view looking towards the buffer stops shows the disused single road engine shed in the middle and the goods shed on the left. The line to the right served the food buffer depot opened in 1939 following the outbreak of World War 2. (C.J.B. Sanderson / ARPT)

29. On the 15th November 1958, the Branch Line Society ran a special train. BR Standard class 2MT 2-6-0 no. 78049 stands in the platform whilst the passengers witness the final rituals of the closure process. (ARPT)

HERIOT

X. Opened on 1st August 1848 the station served a small community close to the main road to Edinburgh (now the A7). It was unusual for the Waverley Route as it had split platforms separated by a level crossing. Heriot became an unstaffed halt from 27th March 1967 and closed with the line on 6th January 1969. Although the reopened line from Tweedbank will pass through the station there are no plans to reopen it. 1907 map at 25" to 1 mile.

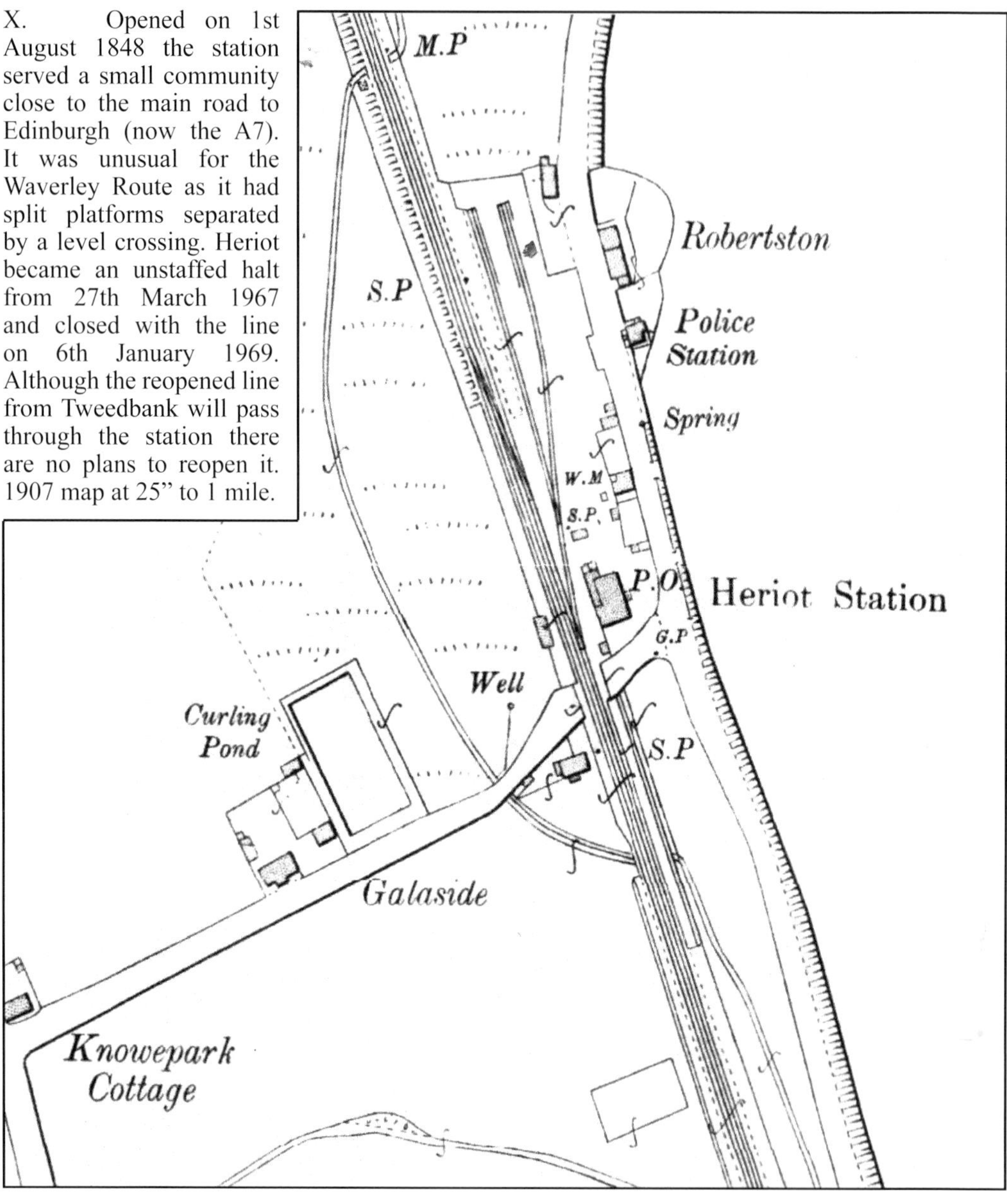

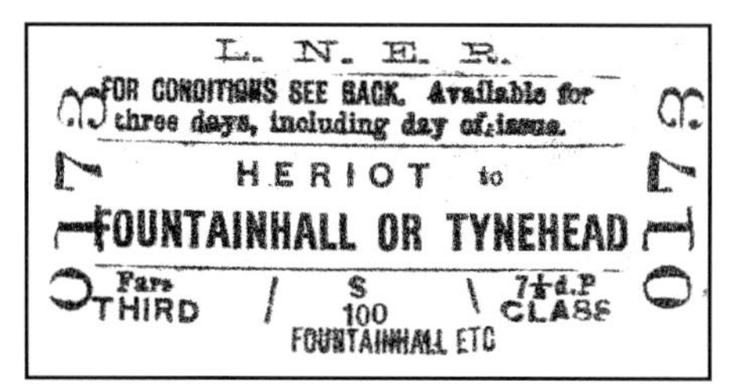

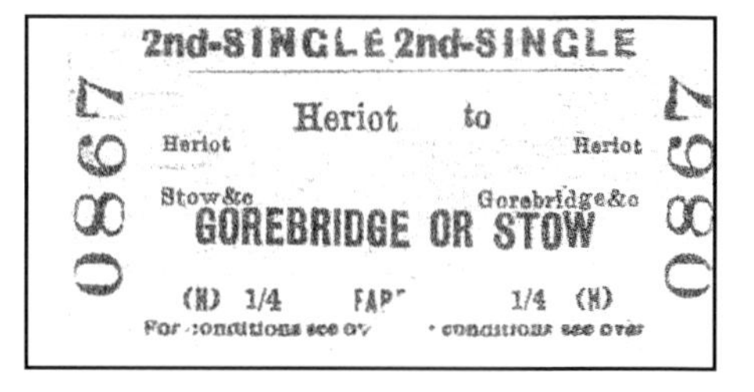

30. The entrance of the station building and the rear of the signal box are seen from the main Edinburgh road (now the A7) with the level crossing separating the two platforms. (J.Alsop coll.)

31. The station building is at ground level opposite the down platform in this 1920s photograph. (Clapperton Trust/J.Alsop coll.)

32. Despite its close proximity to the main Edinburgh road, the area around Heriot station was sparsely populated. A view south towards Fountainhall, shows the trailing point of the down line that gave access to the modest goods facilities. (G.N.Turnbull/R.W.Lynn coll.)

33. A grounded coach stands next to the siding into the goods yard. Meanwhile passengers gather for the approaching train heading for Edinburgh Waverley on 15th May 1954. (C.J.B.Sanderson/ARPT)

34. Class 40 locomotive no. D286 waits with a demolition train in March 1971 whilst the train crew struggle to open what remains of the crossing gates following a snow storm. The line was subject to severe winters on many occasions during its lifetime. (ARPT)

35. Remains of the Up platform were still very much in evidence on 28th February 2008. They will probably disappear as the railway is rebuilt. (D.A.Lovett)

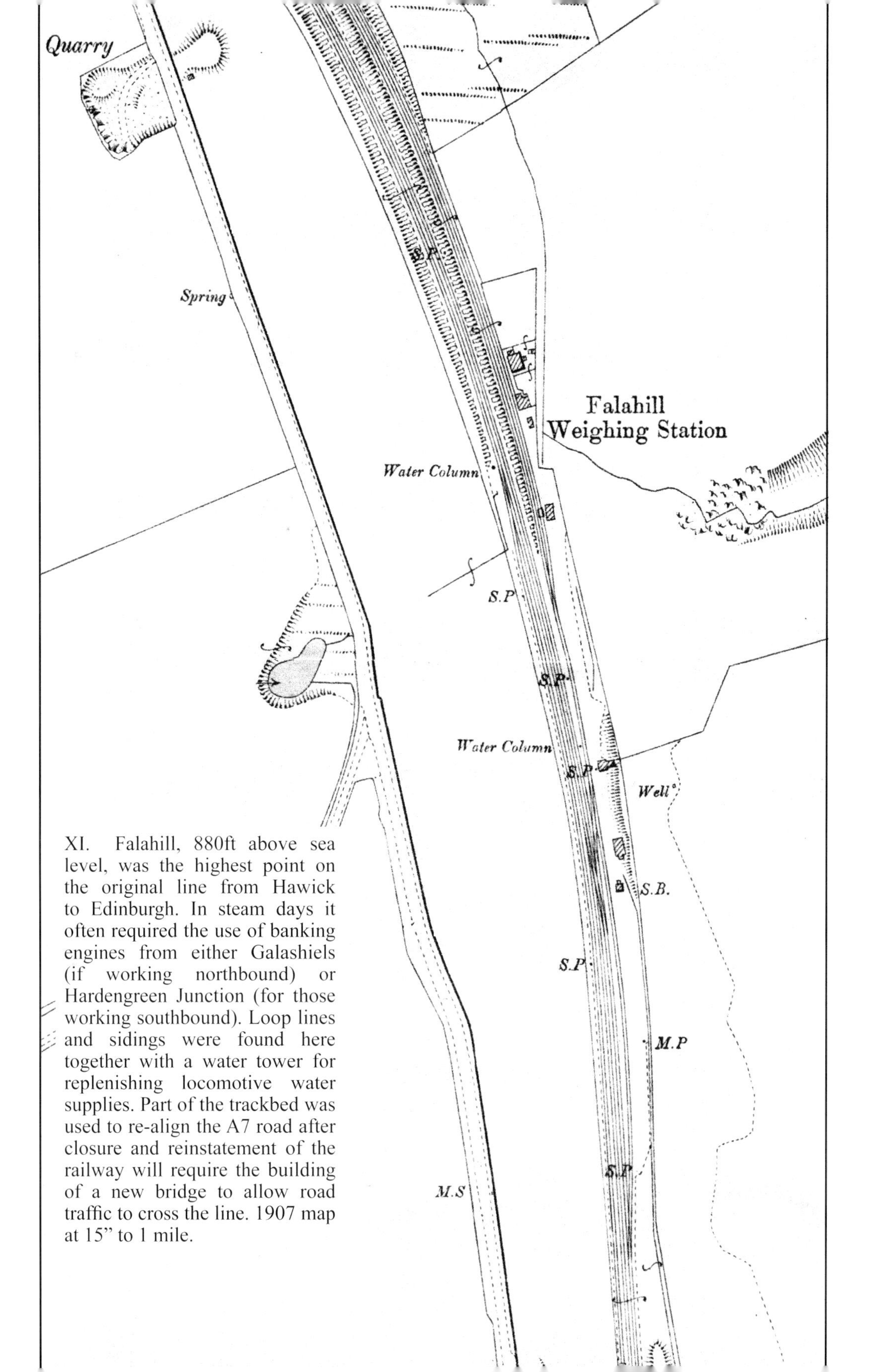

XI. Falahill, 880ft above sea level, was the highest point on the original line from Hawick to Edinburgh. In steam days it often required the use of banking engines from either Galashiels (if working northbound) or Hardengreen Junction (for those working southbound). Loop lines and sidings were found here together with a water tower for replenishing locomotive water supplies. Part of the trackbed was used to re-align the A7 road after closure and reinstatement of the railway will require the building of a new bridge to allow road traffic to cross the line. 1907 map at 15" to 1 mile.

36. B1 Class 4-6-0 no.61308 passes the signal box at Falahill. Built in April 1948 the locomotive was latterly allocated to Thornton Junction in Fife and was withdrawn from there in November 1966. It is seen here on an Edinburgh to Hawick local train. (E.Treacy/R.W.Lynn coll.)

37. In addition to the signal box, this picture gives a good view of the large water tower. A grounded coach body was a welcome refuge for staff who found themselves working at this remote spot. (R.W.Lynn coll.)

38. Class A2 4-6-2 no.60528 *Tudor Minstrel* storms Falahill whilst working the Altrinchamian Railway Excursion Society train between Manchester Exchange and Edinburgh Waverley on 23 April 1966. (A.P.McLean)

39. A4 Class 4-6-2 no.60031 *Golden Plover* climbs Falahill with a south bound train. This locomotive was allocated to Haymarket Depot, Edinburgh for many years before being transferred to St. Rollox, Glasgow. (D.Cross/Colour Rail)

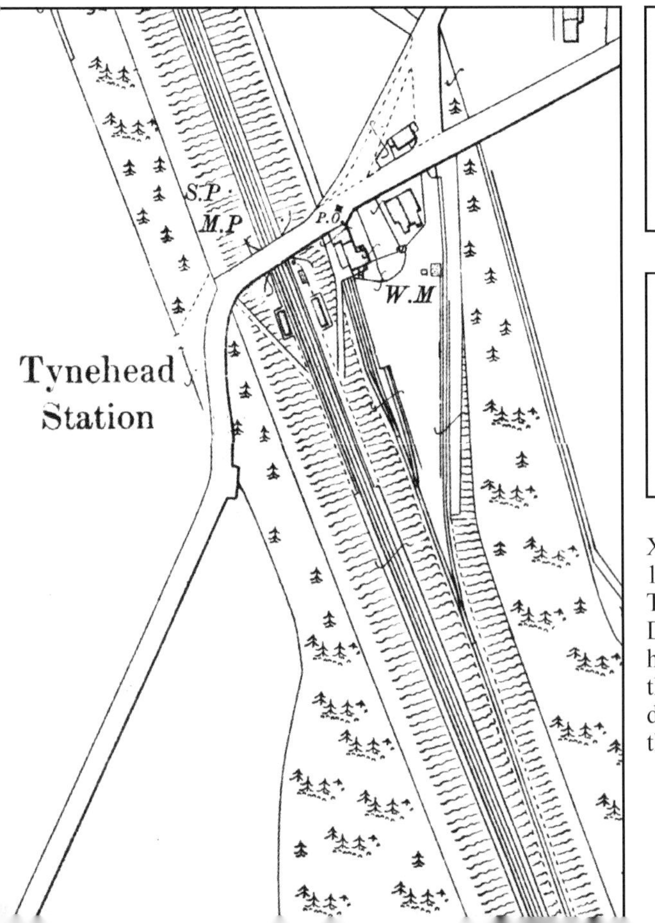

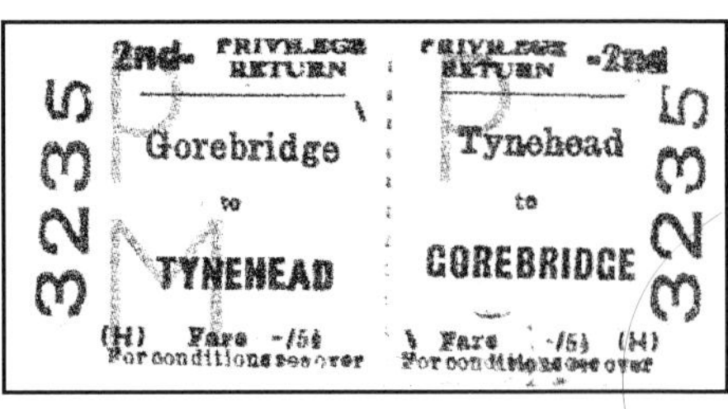

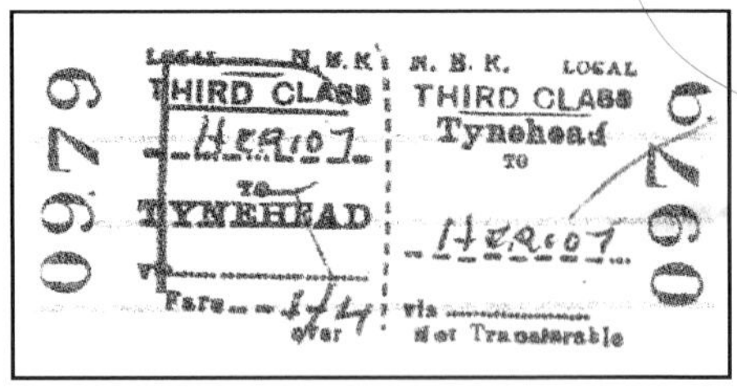

XII. Opened as Tyne Head on 1st August 1848, it became Tynehead in March 1874. The station lost its goods facilities on 28th December 1964 and became an unstaffed halt on 27th March 1967. It closed with the line on 6th January 1969. The station does not feature in the reopening plans for the line. 1907 map at 25" to 1 mile.

40. Tynehead was a split level facility with the goods yard being at a higher level and the station at the lower one. The station was located in a steep cutting with the station building being located to the right of the bridge. (C.J.B.Sanderson/ARPT)

41. Tynehead passengers would need plenty of stamina to reach the road by using the steep pathways. We can only imagine that access to the platforms on cold icy mornings was not as customer friendly as it would need to be today. (C.J.B.Sanderson/ARPT)

42. Track renewal is taking place under the watchful eye of the Tynehead signalman. This is the second box at Tynehead and opened on 12th December 1930. A Clayton Type 1 Bo-Bo diesel (later class 17) locomotive is moving past the engineers train. The smoke and steam is from a rail crane. (N.Forrest/Transport Treasury)

43. The platform shelters are no longer in postion in this view. In the last days of the line, Tynehead had just one call in each direction. The roof of the station building can be seen on the right. (N.Forrest/Transport Treasury)

44. The station building is now a private house. The bridge can be seen and trackbed clearance was very much in evidence when visited on 19th August 2011. (D.A.Lovett)

BORTHWICK BANK

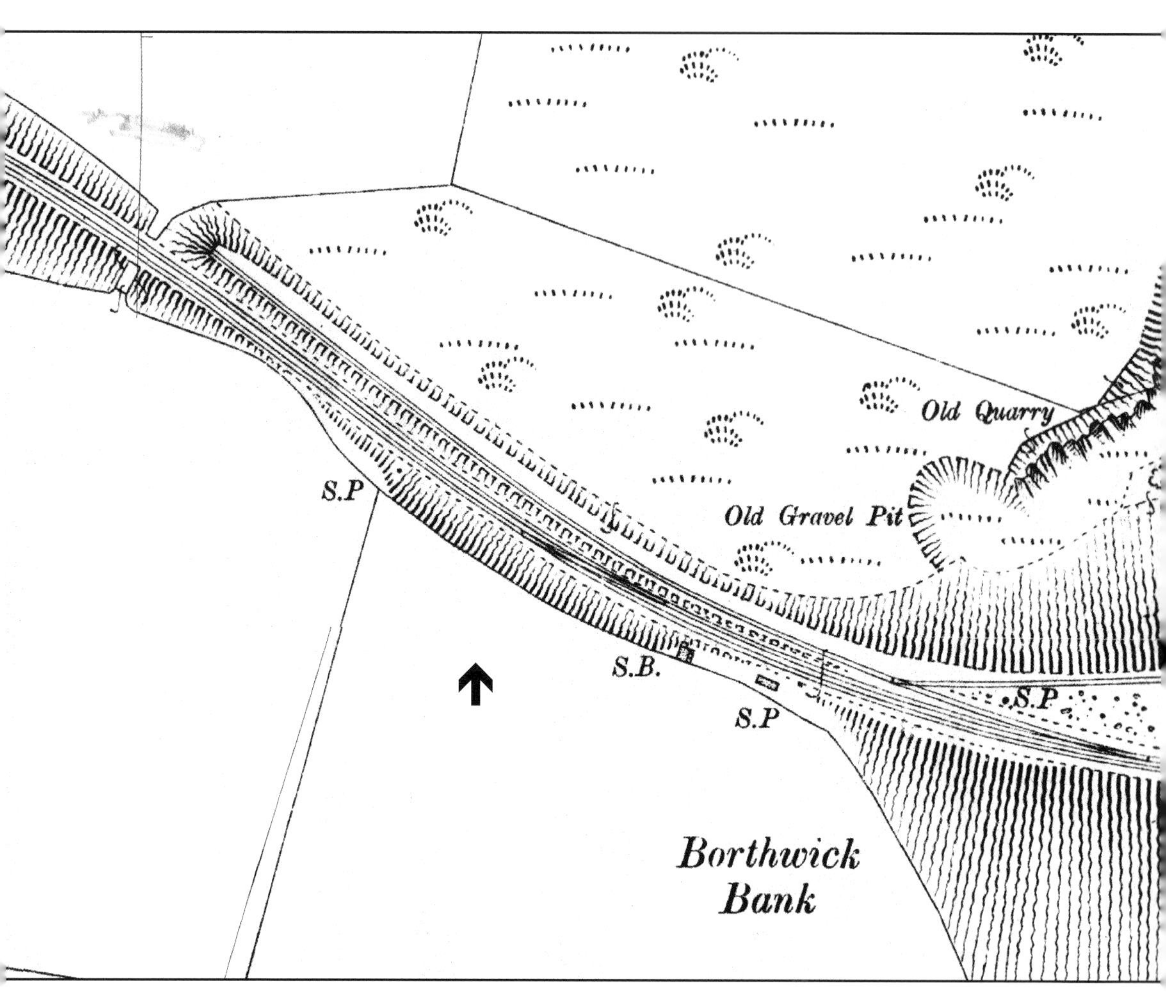

XIII. A siding was provided here for the dumping of ash from St. Margarets engine shed (Edinburgh) in the old gravel pit. The site was also known as Birky Bank or St. Margarets Bank. 1907 map at 25" to 1 mile.

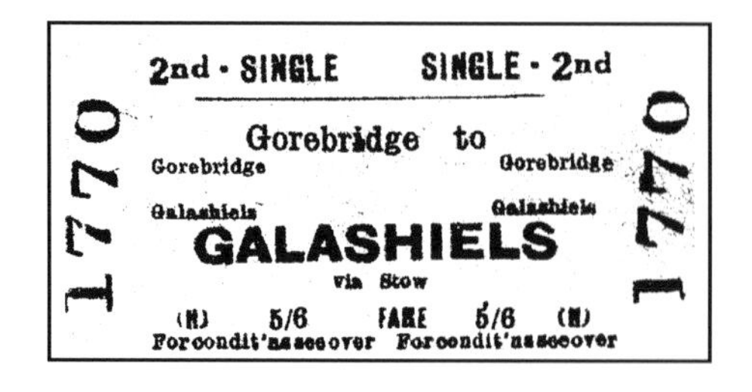

45. The signalman watches the passing of a train. The signal box had 16 levers. (R.W.Lynn coll.)

46. Class 40 1-Co-Co-1 DE no.D263 climbs Borthwick Bank on 20th September 1965. (J.Spencer Gilks/Colour Rail)

XIV. There was a short mineral branch to Esperton Lime Works Quarry, the junction was located south east of Fushiebridge station. Exchange sidings were provided at the junction with the mineral branch. The lime works railway was three miles long and was constructed in 1877/78. The connection with the NBR at Fushiebridge opened on 8th January 1879. (Esperton is spelt elsewhere as Esperston and Esperstone). The lime works had its own locomotives both to work the standard gauge branch and the 2ft 8ins narrow gauge lines in the quarry itself. Early records are not complete but from 1900 onward all the locomotives came from Manning Wardle. In 1936 the quarry lines were relaid to 2ft gauge and operated by Ruston Hornsby 4wDM locomotives. The works closed in 1941 and the equipment was dismantled by 1942. Quarrying again took place in the 1950s and 60s but used road haulage. Sections of the earthworks are still visible and the standard gauge engine shed still stood at Esperton in 2013. The map shows the junction from Fushiebridge and the unusual junction to access the mineral branch. 1893 map at 15" to 1 mile.

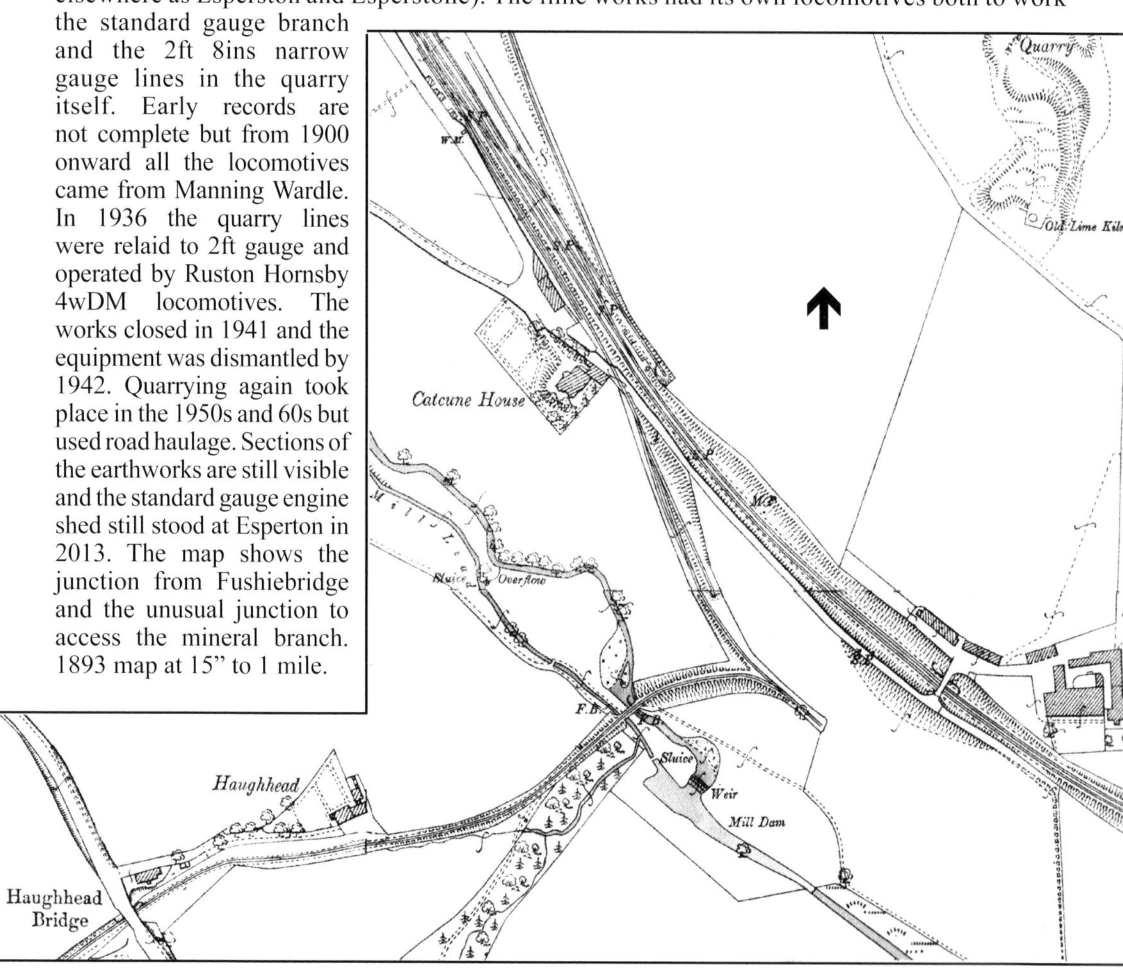

47. Workers pose alongside one of the lightly laid narrow gauge lines within the quarry. This picture dates from the 1880s. (British Geological Survey/NERC.

Licensor www.scran.ac.uk)

FUSHIEBRIDGE

XV. The station first appeared in Bradshaw's in September 1847 as Fushie Bridge, the name it retained until 1877 when it became Fushiebridge. It closed to passengers on 4th October 1943 but remained as a workman's halt to serve the nearby Catcune Mills for some years. Catcune Mills were linked to the Down platform by a footpath. The station also lost its goods facilities on 1st January 1959. A short branch line was built around 1875 to serve Vogrie Colliery via a steep incline and is marked on this 1893 map. Sidings for Vogrie Colliery were on the 'Up' side. The branch was closed and lifted about 1904 but relayed again in 1913 when the colliery reopened. Both colliery and branch closed in 1938. No.1 pit (also known as Jack pit) opened in 1877, no.2 (Mossend or Bryant pit) in 1879, no.3 in 1885 and no.4 in 1889. The latter two were renamed Vogrie 1. The connection to Esperton Limeworks Railway was via a head shunt on the 'Down' side. The station is not scheduled for reopening as part of the Borders Railway project. 1893 map at 25" to 1 mile.

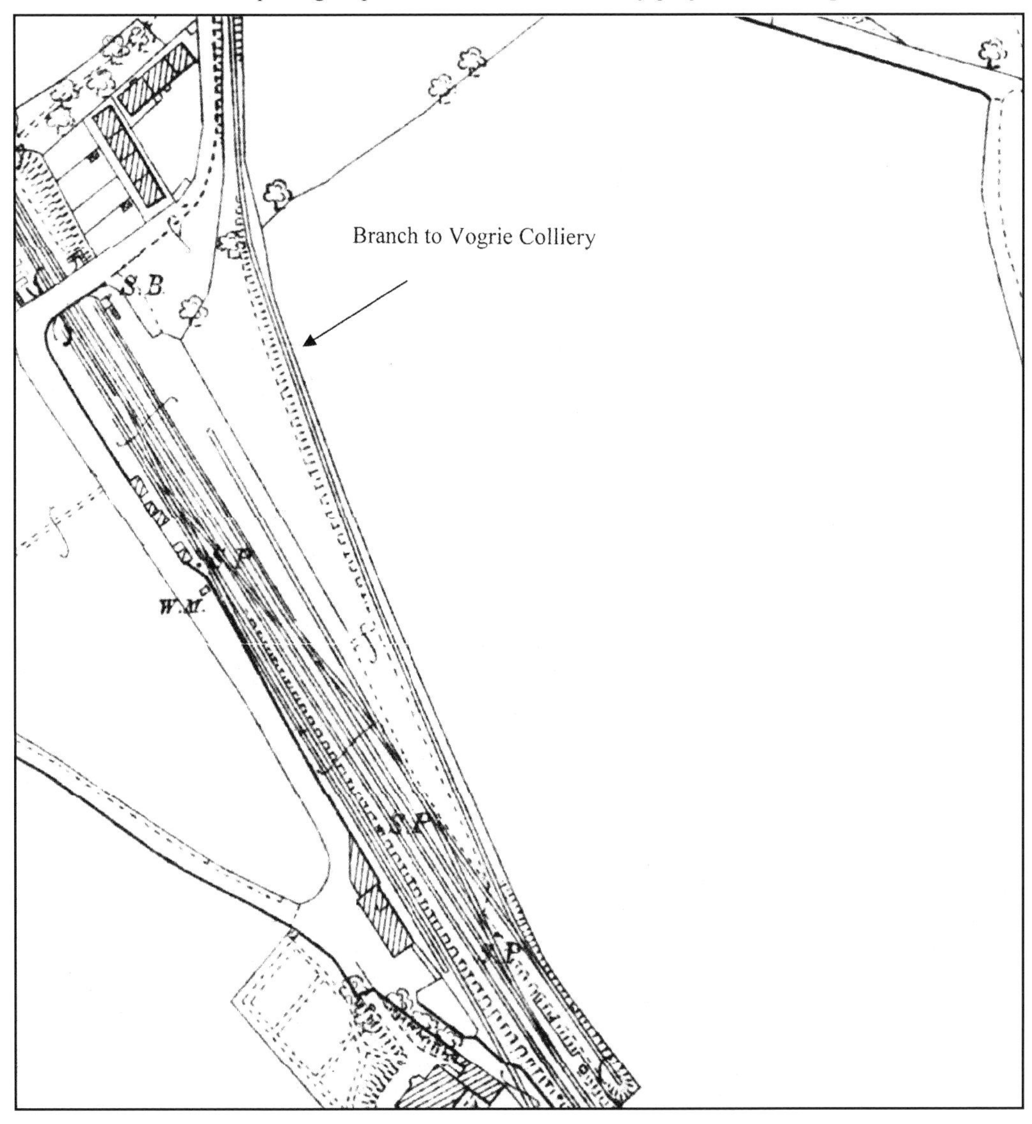

48. Looking north in the 1930s, we can see that work is being carried out on the shelter on the Down platform. (LOSA)

49. A southbound train approaches the now closed station in 1949. The station closed in 1943 to regular passenger traffic but continued for some years as a halt for workers employed at the nearby Catcune Mill. (R.W.Lynn coll.)

50. The platforms had been removed when this photograph was taken and fenced off. The station building remained in good order despite the lack of potential passengers when photographed on 15th May 1954. (C.J.B. Sanderson / ARPT)

51 Class 26 Bo-Bo DE no.D5304 heads south pass the signal box in July 1963. The remains of the station can be seen in the background behind the last coach. (K.M.Falconer/Colour Rail)

GOREBRIDGE

XVI. Opened on 14th July 1847 as Gore Bridge, it bacame Gorebridge in 1872. The station had staggered platforms with the small goods yard at the south end. There was no covered goods shed but a 2-ton capacity crane was provided. The station became an unstaffed halt on 27th March 1967 and closed with the line on the 6th January 1969. The goods yard closed on 28th December 1964. In 2011 Gorebridge had a population of 5,777. The station is to be rebuilt on the current site as part of the reopened Borders Railway. 1907 map at 25" to 1 mile.

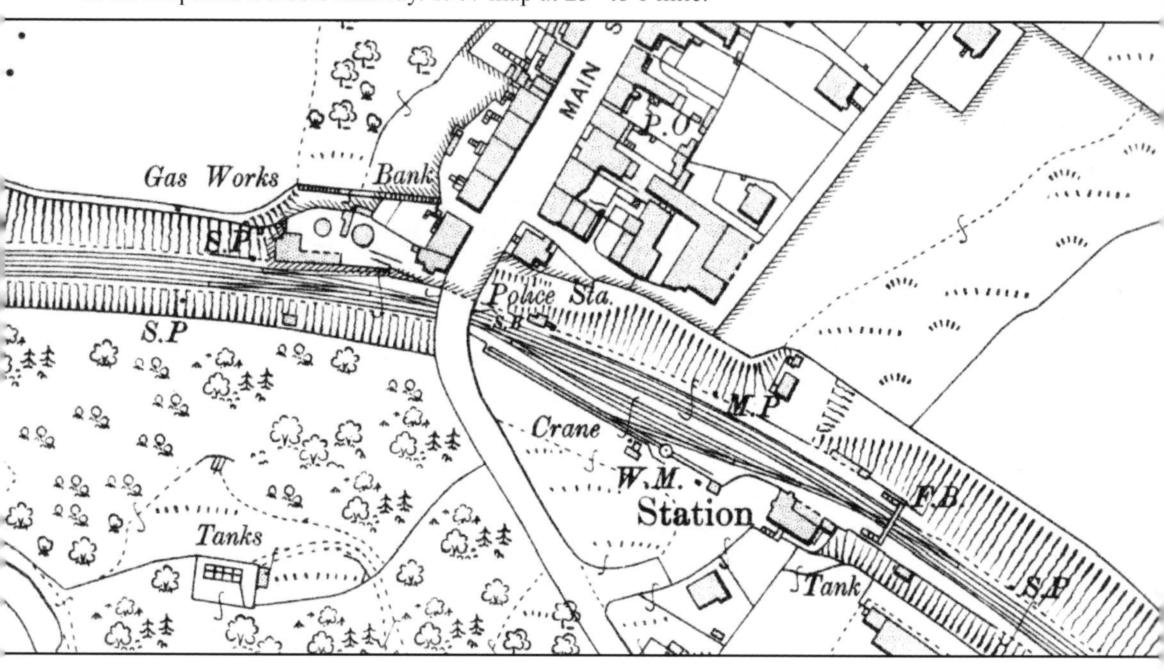

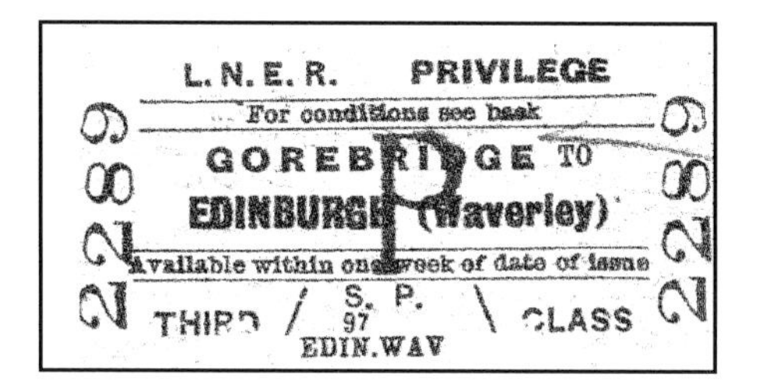

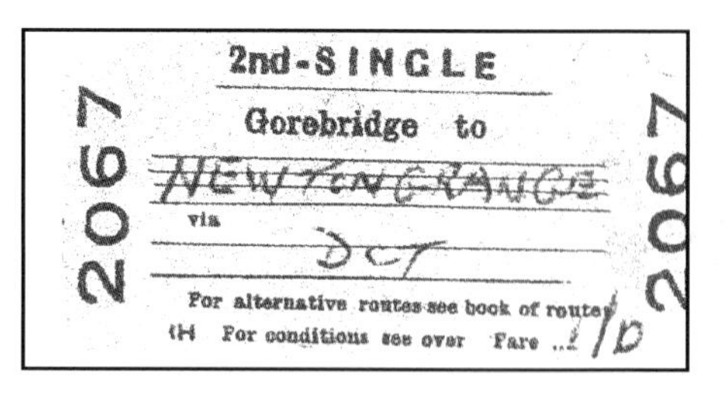

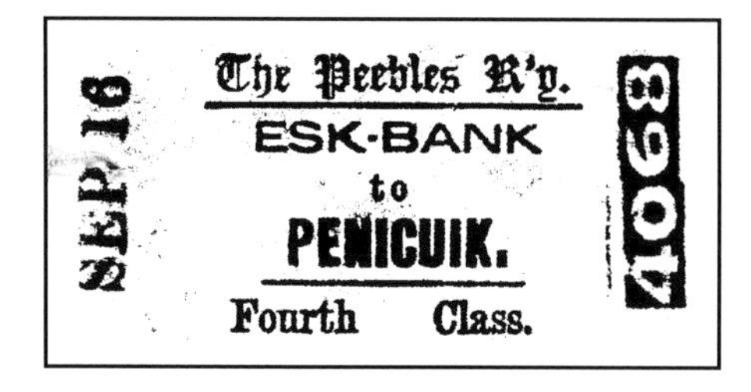

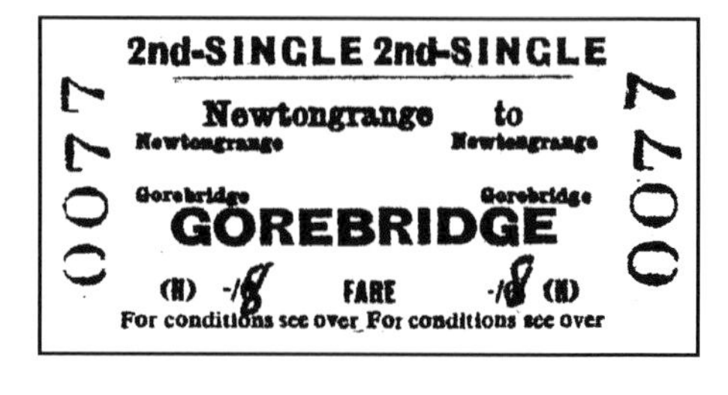

52. We are looking south on 15th May 1954, with the station building on the right and the staggered platforms are linked by the footbridge. The goods yard sat to the south of the main building with the access tracks to the sidings visible on the right. (C.J.B.Sanderson/ARPT)

53. Looking north on the same day, we see the slip point into the goods yard is controlled from the signal box on the down platform in the distance. The road bridge from the town crosses over the line and still remains today. Houses were built on the trackbed and these have been demolished for the restored railway. (C.J.B.Sanderson/ARPT)

54. Gresley designed K3 Class 2-6-0 no.61885 heads from Millerhill through the station with a freight train on 15th May 1954. (C.J.B.Sanderson/ARPT)

55. The former station building was for a period a restaurant known as Porters. It was photographed on 19th August 2011 before work on rebuilding the line had begun. (D.A.Lovett)

ARNISTON COLLIERY

XVII. Arniston Colliery comprised two pits, Emily and Gore. Emily opened in 1858 and Gore twenty years later. Owned by the Arniston Coal Company, they became part of the National Coal Board in 1947. The pits were served by a short branch line and closed in 1962. This map shows the complexity of industrial lines between Fushiebridge and Hardengreen Junction around 1900. (A.E.Young)

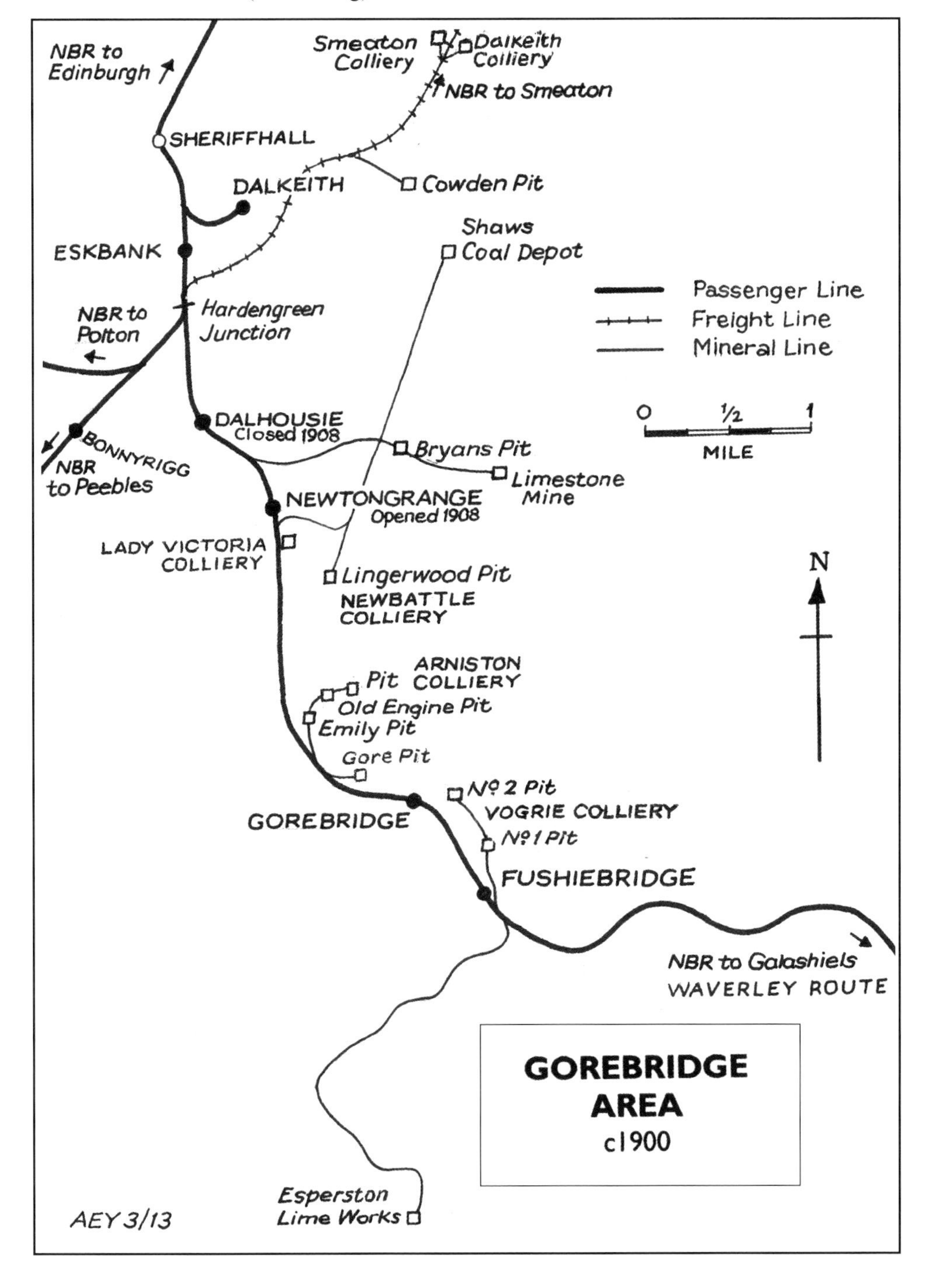

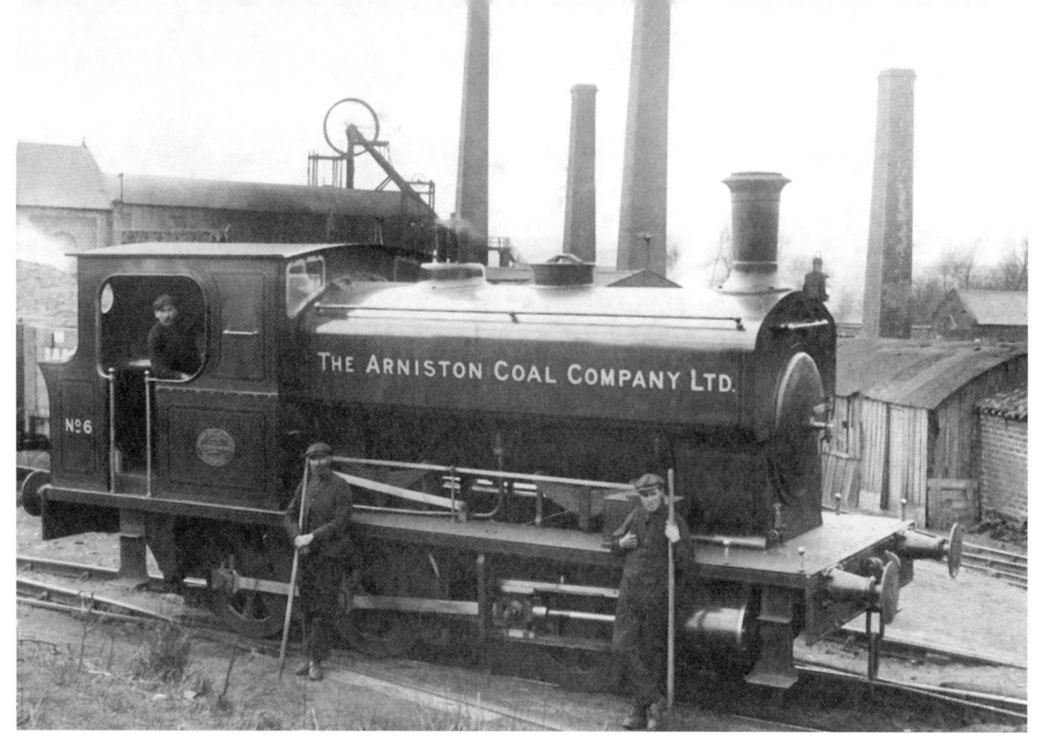

56. The Arniston Coal Company 0-6-0ST was Andrew Barclay works no.1233 of 1911. It was new to the coal company. In NCB days it was renumbered 9. By 1967 it was based at Niddrie Locomotive Shed where it was scrapped in September 1969. It is seen here at the northwest end of Emily Pit sidings with the kilns of the brickyard behind it.
(National Mining Museum Scotland Trust coll.)

The National Mining Museum Scotland would appreciate any further details about these photographs, their dates and photographers.

57. Class V2 2-6-2 no.60873 *Coldstreamer* on a down train approaches Gore Pit, Arniston Colliery and the exchange sidings. The railway closed in 1962, the washery in 1963 and the sidings were removed about 1965, which helps to date the photograph.
(National Mining Museum Scotland Trust coll.)

LADY VICTORIA COLLIERY

XVIII. Known as Newbattle Colliery, production commenced in 1895. Colliery sidings could take 411 wagons. In 1912 it was agreed that both NBR and colliery locomotives could work in the sidings at the same time but in 1913 two sidings off the Waverley Route were built so that trains could be marshalled by the Lothian Coal Co and then picked up by the NBR as full train from these exchange sidings. Owned by the Lothian Coal Co. it passed to the National Coal Board on nationalisation in 1947. Coal production reached its peak in 1953 when 1,765 were employed at the pit. Closed in 1981 and abandoned a year later, Lady Victoria survives today as the Scottish Mining Museum. 1907 map is at 15" to 1 mile.

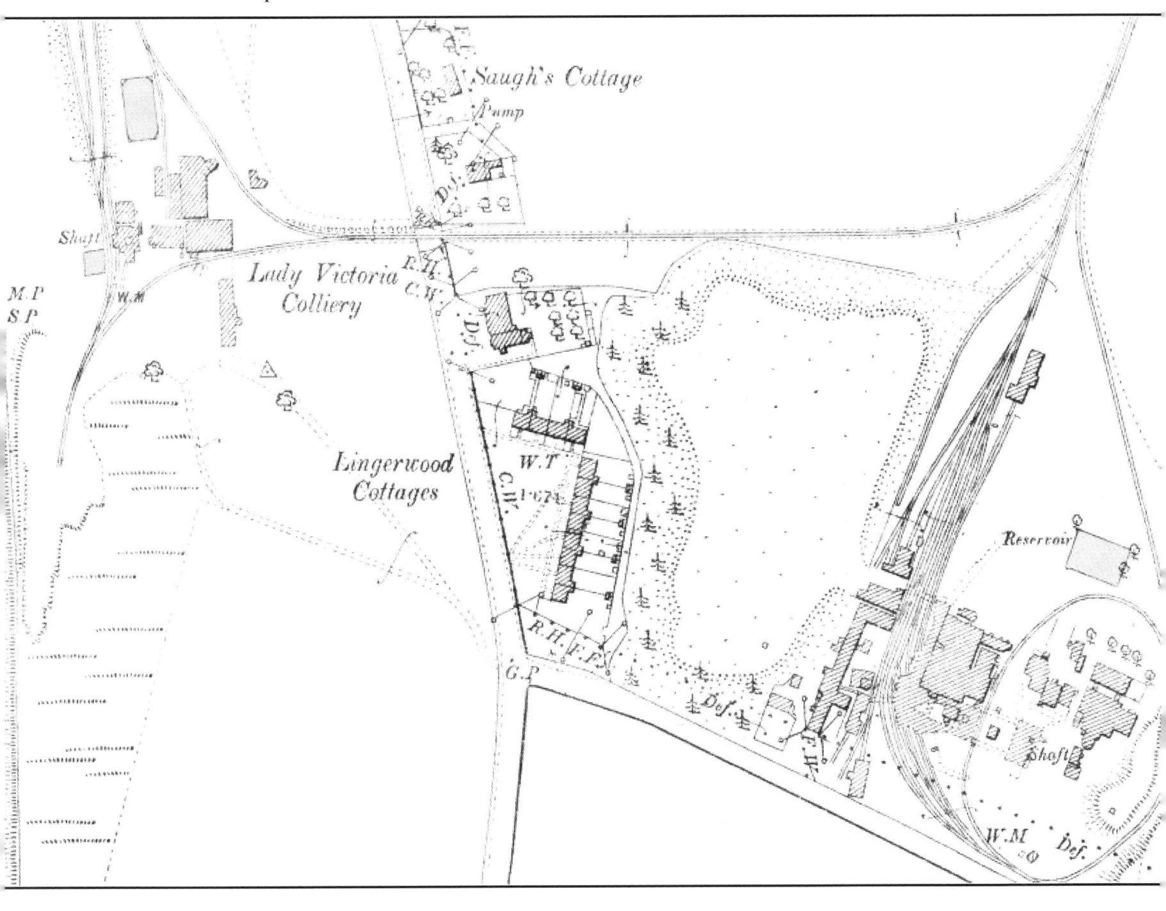

58. The signal box was located at the south end of the complex adjacent to the Waverley line. It controlled access to and from the exchange sidings from the main line. (R.W. Lynn coll.)

59. Andrew Barclay supplied 0-4-0ST No.2 new to Lady Victoria in 1902 as their no.928 and it was rebuilt at Newbattle in 1931. It is seen shunting wagons ready for loading in 1969. It was scrapped on site in September of that year. (J. Furnevel)

60. Taken from the south end of the colliery complex on 6th October 1971, this photograph is looking towards Netwtongrange station. The Waverley route is on the left. (J. Furnevel)

61. NCB locomotive 0-4-0ST no.2 was shunting at Lady Victoria colliery in 1969. This picture gives a closer view of the overhead loading plant and hopper discharge. (J. Furnevel)

62. The first ever Scottish Railway Preservation Society railtour 'The Edinburgh Rambler' visited the site on the 23rd May 1970. Class 20 Bo-BoDE no.D8102 is being assisted by one of the resident 0-4-2ST engines. Scottish coal companies favoured the 0-4-2ST arrangement. (A.P. McLean)

63. Grant, Ritchie & Co. 0-4-2T locomotive NCB no. 7 was built in Townholme Engine Works, Kilmarnock with works no.596 1914. It spent most of its working life at Lady Victoria but was at Arniston between 1954 and 1957 and was seen at Lady Victoria in 1971. It went to Prestongrange Industrial Heritage Museum in 1975 where it remains. (ARPT)

64. A train of internal user wagons heads under the distinctive overhead weighouse at Lady Victoria colliery on 6th October 1971. (J. Furneval)

65. Lady Victoria Colliery is home to the National Mining Museum of Scotland and is a popular visitor attraction. The museum complex is seen here on 13th October 2008. (D.A.Lovett)

NEWTONGRANGE

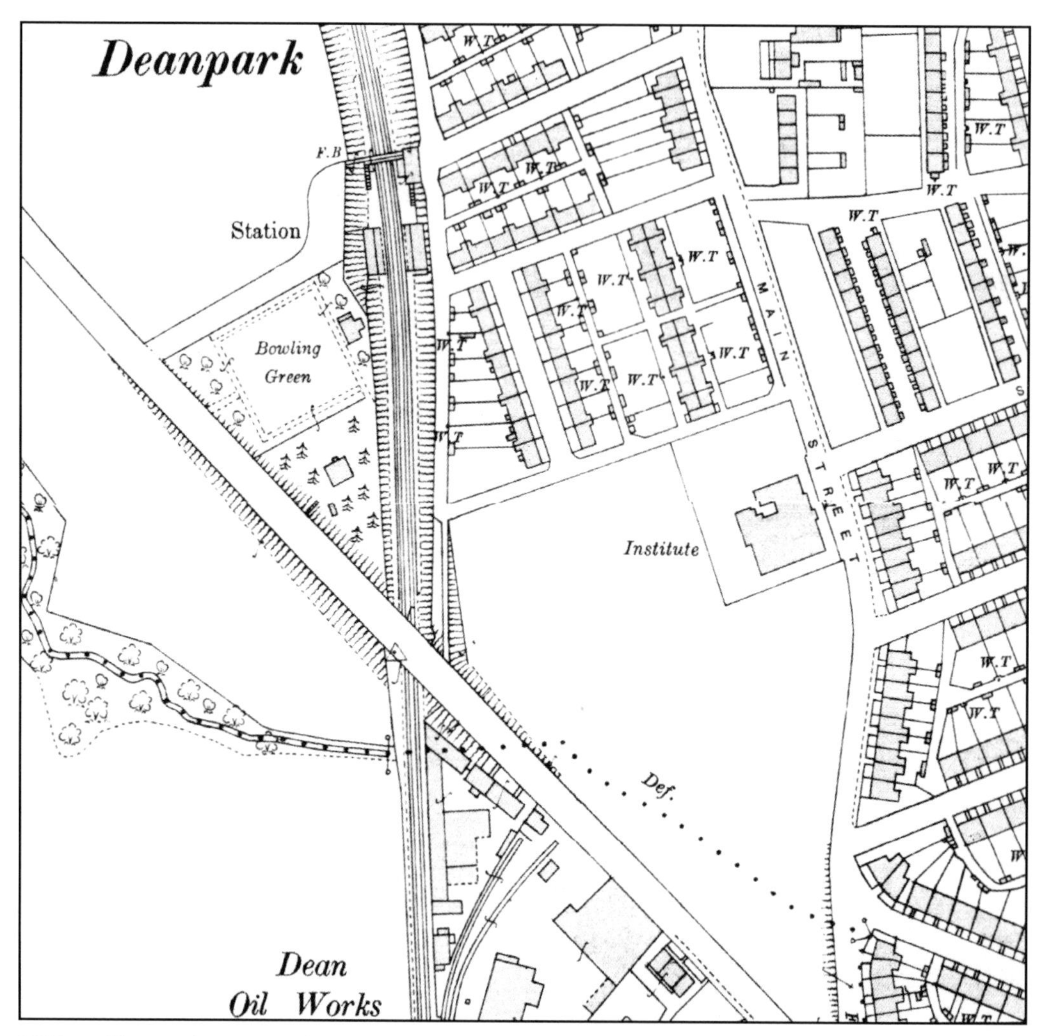

XIX. The station opened on 1st August 1908 and replaced Dalhousie. The main Edinburgh road (now the A7) crossed the line at the south end of the station. Because it was built late, the site was restricted and no goods facilities were provided. It became an unstaffed halt on 5th December 1960 and closed with the line on 6th January 1969. The town was a mining community with many of the residents being employed at local collieries such as Lady Victoria. As part of the Borders Railway project a new station was planned south of the A7 bridge on cleared land. 1914 map at 25" to 1 mile.

L.N.E.R. For conditions see back. L.N.E.R. For conditions see back.
719 PRIVILEGE TICKET Valid 7 Days Third Class Single PRIVILEGE TICKET Valid 7 Days Third Class Single 719
Newtongrange Newtongrange
Newtongrange To
EDINBURGH (WAVERLEY)
Edin-(Wav-) Edin-(Wav-)

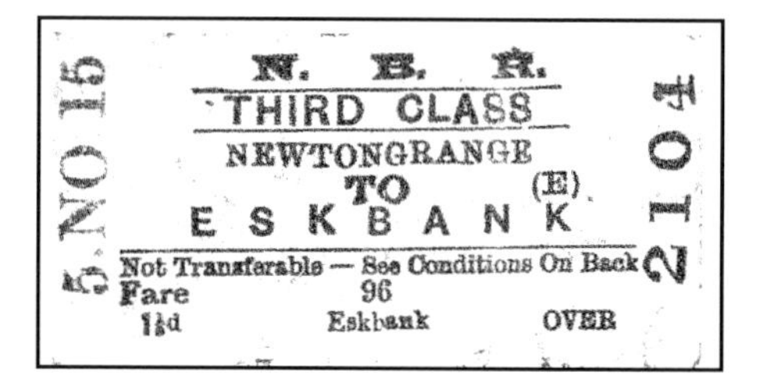
5 NO 15
N. B. R.
THIRD CLASS
NEWTONGRANGE
TO (E)
ESKBANK
Not Transferable — See Conditions On Back
Fare 96
1½d Eskbank OVER
2104

66. In this view dated August 1908, the photographer is looking north with the main station building on the right. The station was in a cutting and access was gained through the booking office. Large shelters were provided on both platforms.(J.Alsop coll.)

67. The shelters have been removed allowing the access arrangements from the booking hall to be clearly seen. The new station will meet the requirements of the Disability Discrimination Act which the old one clearly did not! (K. Norris /R.W.Lynn coll.)

68. A visit on 19th August 2011 found advanced works taking place on the site of the new station. The photographer was standing on the A7 road bridge looking towards Lady Victoria Colliery. (D.A.Lovett)

LOTHIAN BRIDGE

XX. Lothian Bridge is the site of Newbattle Viaduct which comprised of 23 arches over its length of 1,200ft. Built by Grainger & Miller, Engineers to NBR over the River South Esk, 80ft above the river it comprises 14 spans of 39ft, 7 spans of 38ft, 1 of 44ft and 1 of 43ft 10 ins the eastern most arch over the A7 being a skew arch. This replaced the Marquess of Lothian's 1830 bridge of 1,200 ft at a height of 70ft with 3 cast iron arches of 65ft and the latter was demolished. It is a Grade B listed structure and is being restored as part of the reopening of the Borders Railway to Tweedbank from Edinburgh. The sidings to the northeast were part of the Newbattle Brick & Tile Company. 1907 map at 25" to 1 mile.

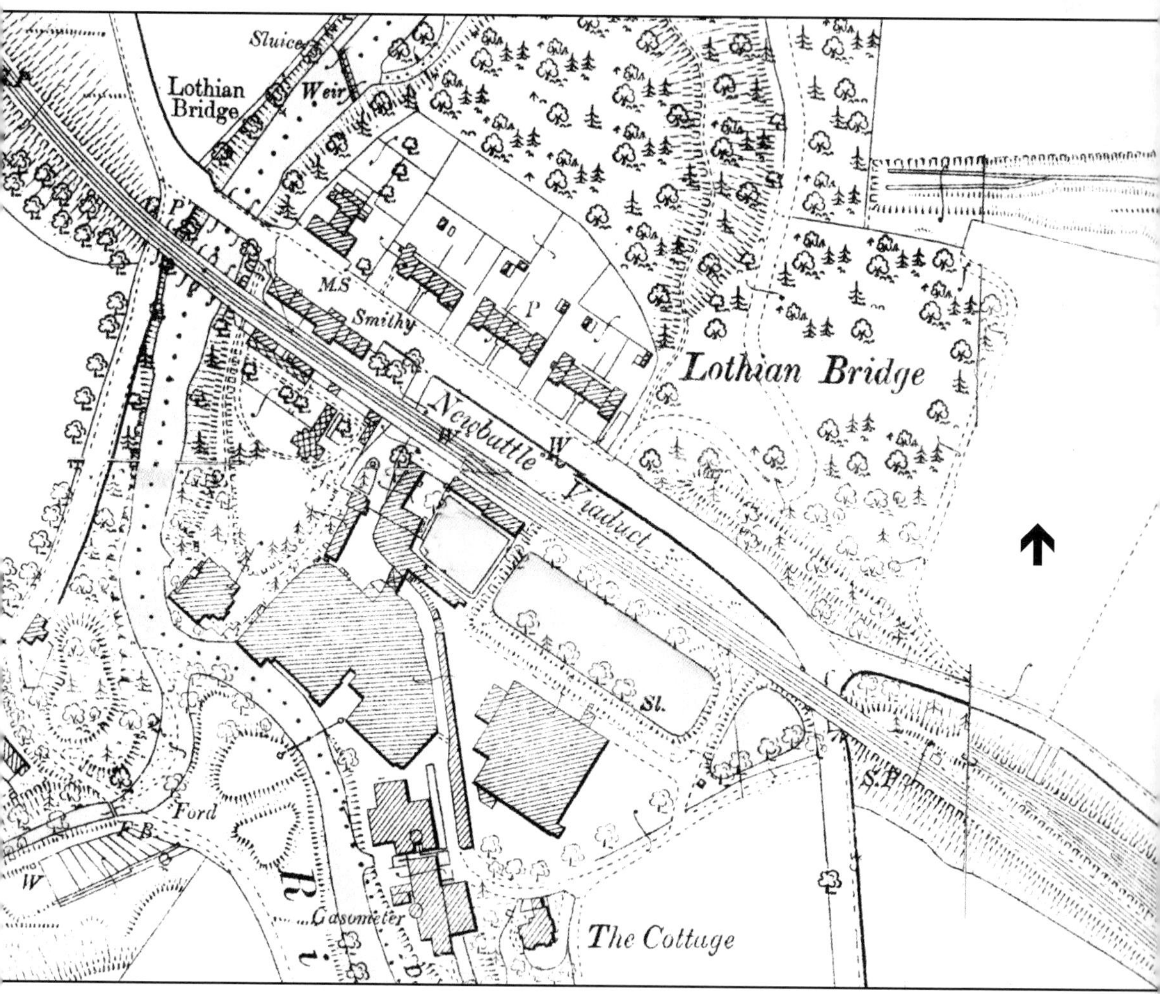

69. Two Clayton Bo-Bo diesels (later Class 17) work across Newbattle Viaduct with a down goods on 11th July 1964. The A7 road passes left to right across the picture with the road from Dalkeith joining it at the junction. The Pentland Hills dominate the background. (R.Montgomery)

70. Taken on 19th August 2011 before renovation work had begun, the impressive Newbattle Viaduct had plenty of vegetation growing on the trackbed. The main A7 road having run parallel with the line then swings sharply to the right. The photographer is standing on the road leading from Dalkeith which is also seen in the picture above. (D.A.Lovett)

DALHOUSIE

XXI. Opened as South Esk on 2nd June 1832, the station was renamed Dalhousie on 12th July 1847. It closed on 1st August 1908 when it was replaced by a new station at Newtongrange. Dalhousie siding closed to goods traffic on 23rd March 1964 and was an unstaffed public siding at closure. 1893 map at 25" to 1 mile.

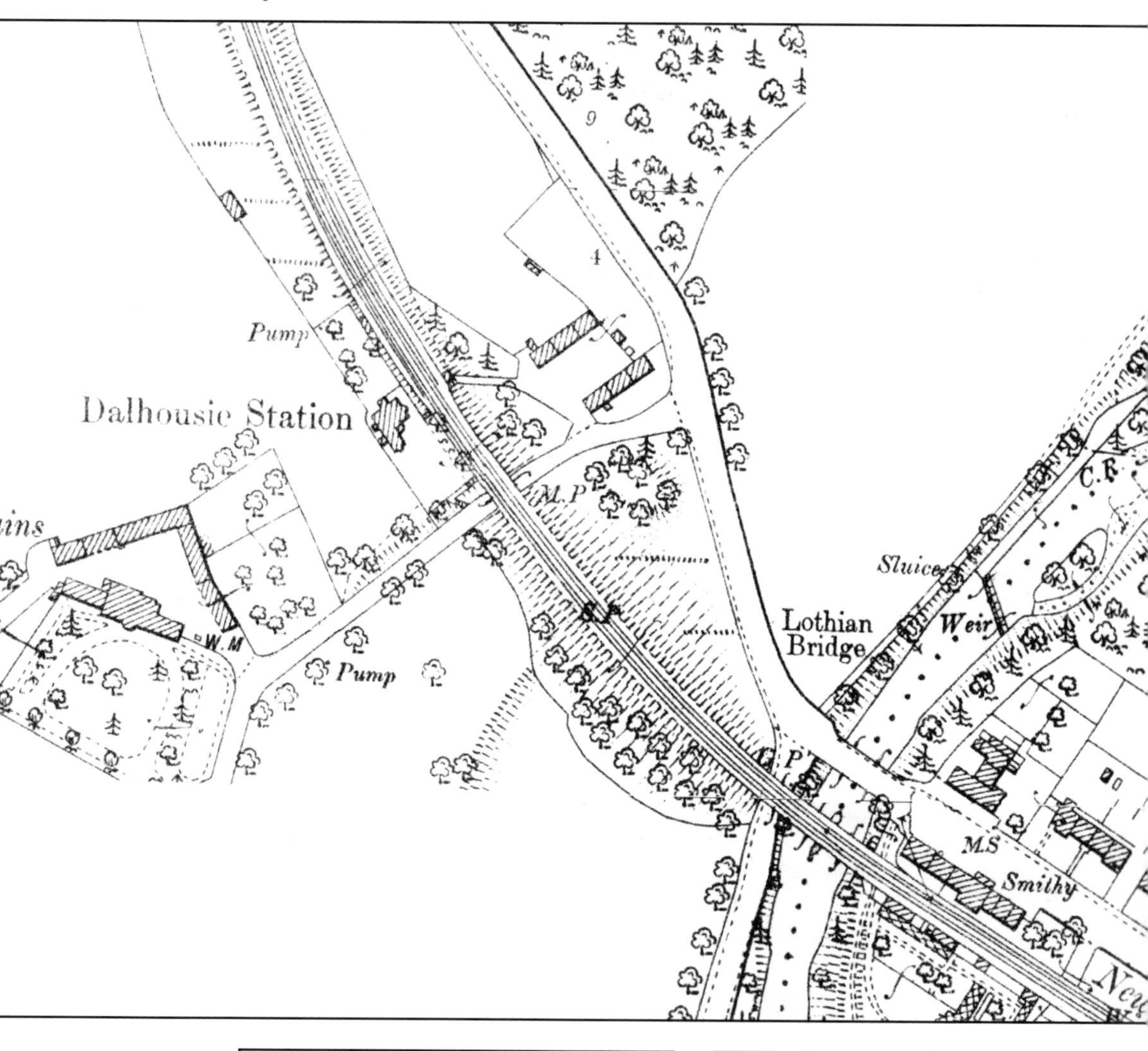

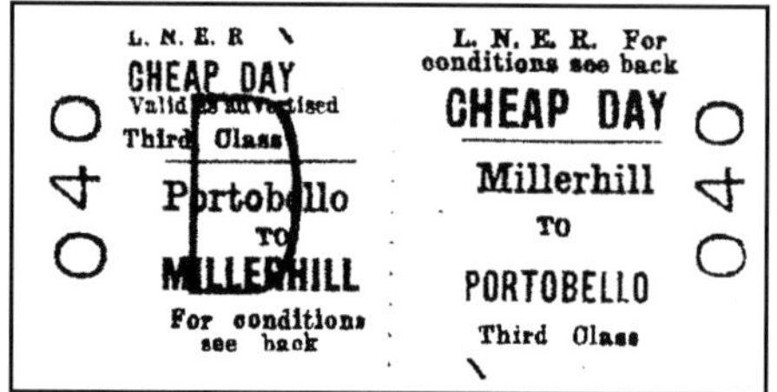

71. The station building combined the ticket office and the stationmasters house set back from the platforms which were removed rapidly after closure. (W.N.Munro/R.W.Lynn coll.)

72. Class A3 4-6-2 no.60043 *Brown Jack* heads the 4.30pm Carlisle to Millerhill freight train past the site of Dalhousie platforms on 19th June 1963. (R.Montgomery)

HARDENGREEN JUNCTION

XXII. The line from Peebles which later provided an alternative route from Galashiels to Edinburgh rejoined the Waverley route at Hardengreen Junction. This line was opened by the Peebles Railway between Peebles and Hardengreen on 4th July 1855, Peebles originally being a terminus. The line between Galashiels and Peebles did not open until 1866. The Peebles line closed to all traffic on 3rd February 1962. A further branch from this line served Penicuik from Hawthornden Junction and this line remained open to goods traffic until 25th March 1967. With the demise of this traffic the last remnants of the Peebles Railway were removed. An alternative line to serve the Dalkeith area pits and to connect them at Smeaton with the Macmerry and Gifford branches opened on 31st July 1870. The line was, however, mothballed in 1913 and was closed and lifted in 1934 with the exception of two short stubs at each end. The goods yard closed on 22nd July 1968, there being no passenger facilities whatsoever. 1893 map at 15" to 1 mile.

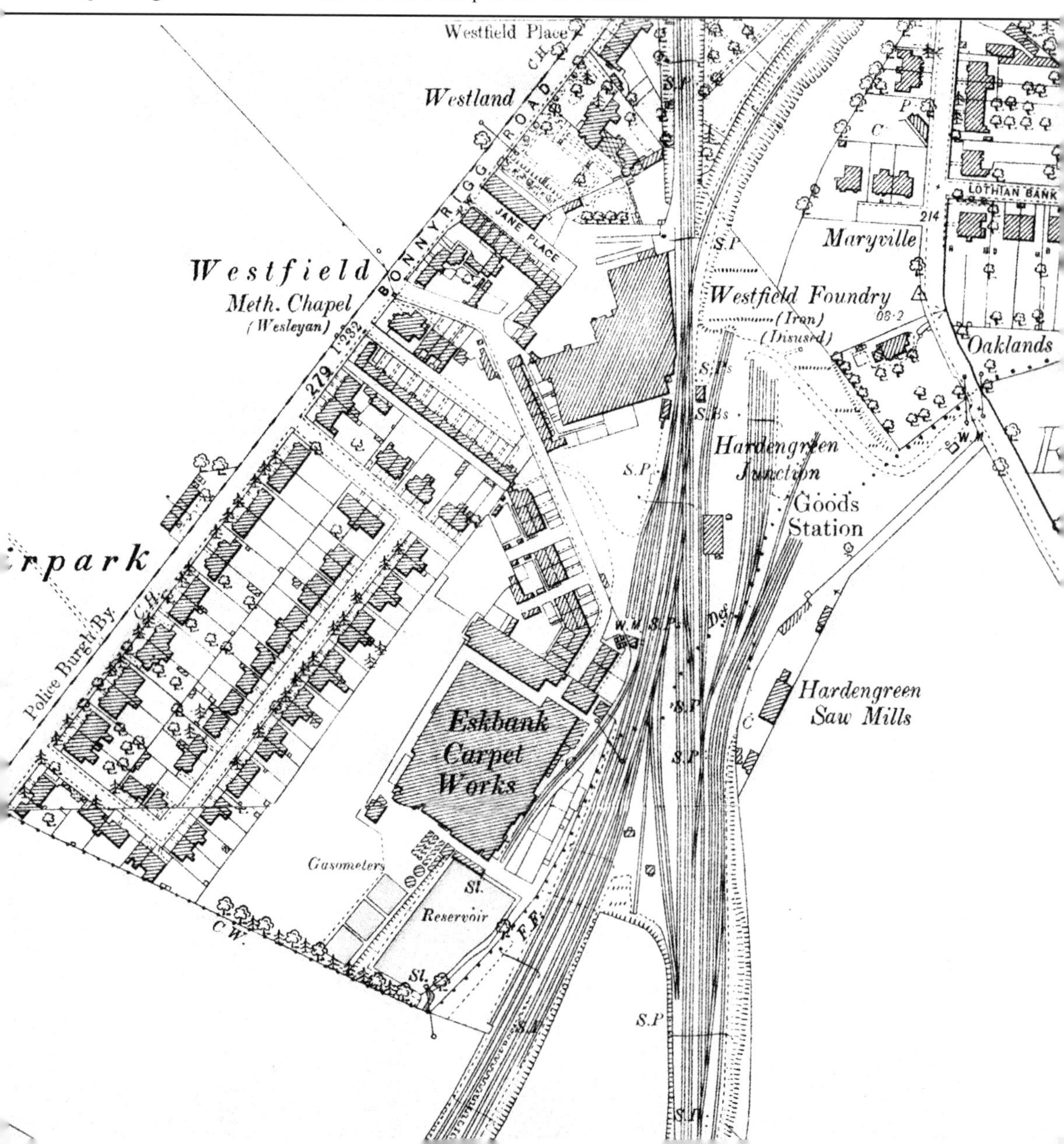

73. The impressive signal box at Hardengreen controlled the branch lines to Peebles and to Smeaton as well as the goods yard and locomotive facilities. (R.W.Lynn coll.)

74. Former LMS Black 5 4-6-0 no. 44884 passes Hardengreen box on an up Special on 14th June 1963. The picture has been taken from the up Peebles line. (R.Montgomery)

75. The locomotive facility here was somewhat minimal and opened when banking over Falahill began. It comprised of an open-air servicing pit and coaling stage. There are no indications that a shed building was ever provided. The facility was, like Galashiels, a sub-shed of St. Margarets, Edinburgh with its main work being to provide banking engines for the climb to Falahill. It also provided locomotives for hauling coal trains from the Dalkeith area collieries. The facility closed on 21st July1962. J38 and J39 locomotives were not diagrammed for here as their tenders were too high for the hand coaling siding. NBR Class C (LNER J36) no.65334 awaits its next turn of duty at Hardengreen on 3rd September 1960. The coaling stage can be seen in the background. (R.Montgomery)

ESKBANK & DALKEITH

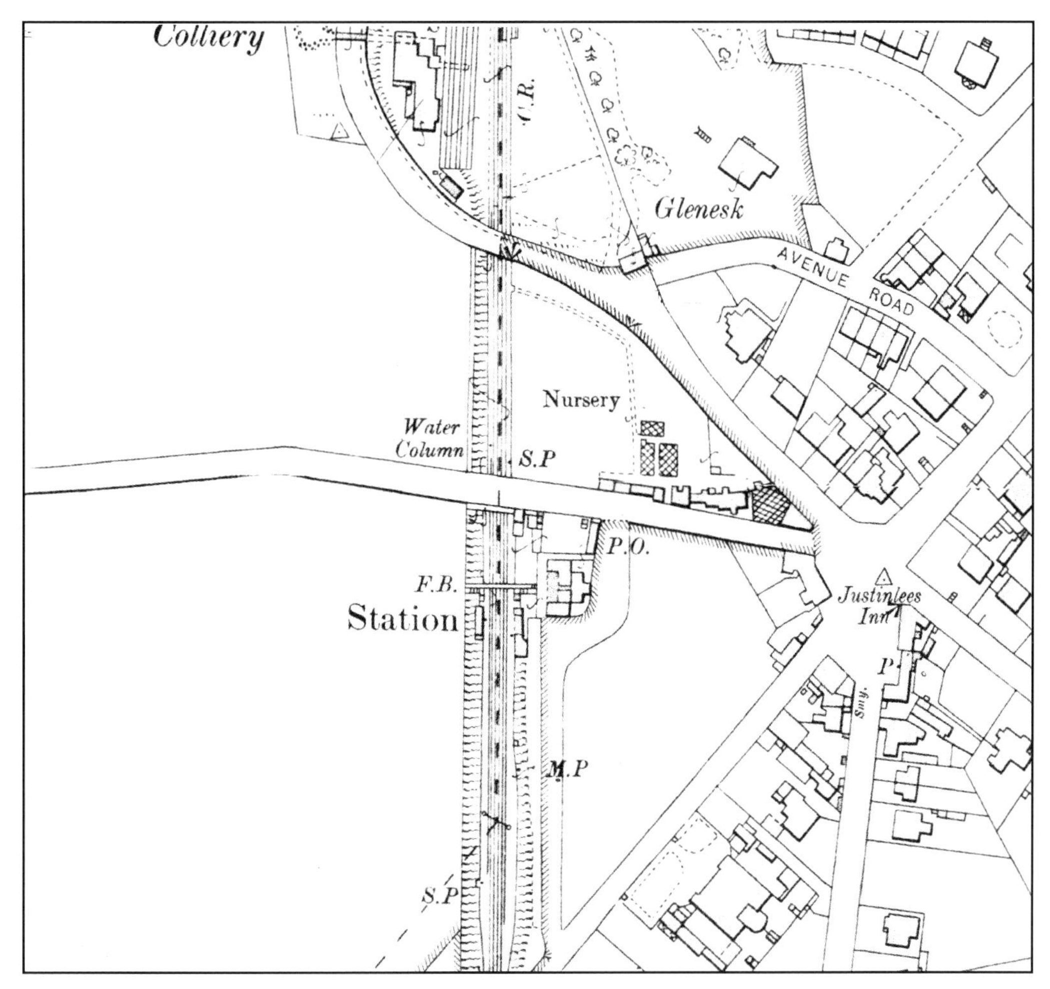

XXIII. Opened as Gallowshall in July 1849, the station was renamed Eskbank in 1850. After closure of the Dalkeith branch to passenger traffic in 1942 it was renamed Eskbank & Dalkeith in 1951. It became an unstaffed halt from 27th March 1967 and closed with the line on 6th January 1969. No goods facilities were provided as these were located at Hardengreen Junction to the south of the station. 1907 map at 25" to 1 mile.

2nd-PRIVILEGE SINGLE | PRIVILEGE-2nd SINGLE
3747
Eskbank & Dalkeith to
Eskbank&D. | Eskbank&D
Edinburgh(Waverley) | Edinburgh(Waverley)
EDINBURGH (WAVERLEY)
(H) -/6 FARE -/6 (H)
For conditions see over | For conditions see over
3747

3rd-SINGLE | SINGLE-3rd
754
Eskbank To
Eskbank | Eskbank
N'tongrange&c | Millerhill&c
MILLERHILL OR NEWTONGRANGE
(H) -/4 H FARE -/4 H (H)
ForConditions see over | ForConditions see over
754

76. A tall NBR lattice signal gives a clear road north. The station buildings are again on top of the bank with the platforms in the cutting. (R.W.Lynn coll.)

77. A platform view in the same direction shows the waiting rooms at the north end of the platform and the length of the station nameboard! (C.J.B.Sanderson/ARPT)

78. A Gloucester Twin DMU (later BR Class 100) picks up passengers for Edinburgh Waverley in 1965. Light blue and white BR Scottish Region nameboards have replaced the old NBR boards. (A.P.McLean)

79. A 1965 view from the Up platform looks towards Edinburgh. Trains will once again serve the local community after reopening in 2015, although the station will not be on the same site but will be near the Dalkeith campus of Edinburgh College. (A.P.McLean)

80. The impressive restored station house and adjacent booking office are seen on 12th April 2010. The booking office was linked to the platforms below by a footbridge. The buildings are now a private residence. (D.A.Lovett)

81. On 12th April 2010 the overgrown platforms and disused footbridge remained in place whilst the main trackbed served as a footpath. The footbridge has now been donated to the Waverley Route Heritage Centre based at Whitrope (see our *Carlisle to Hawick* and *Hexham to Hawick* albums). A new station on a different site near the Tesco Superstore to the south was planned as part of the Borders Railway project. (D.A.Lovett)

GLENESK JUNCTION

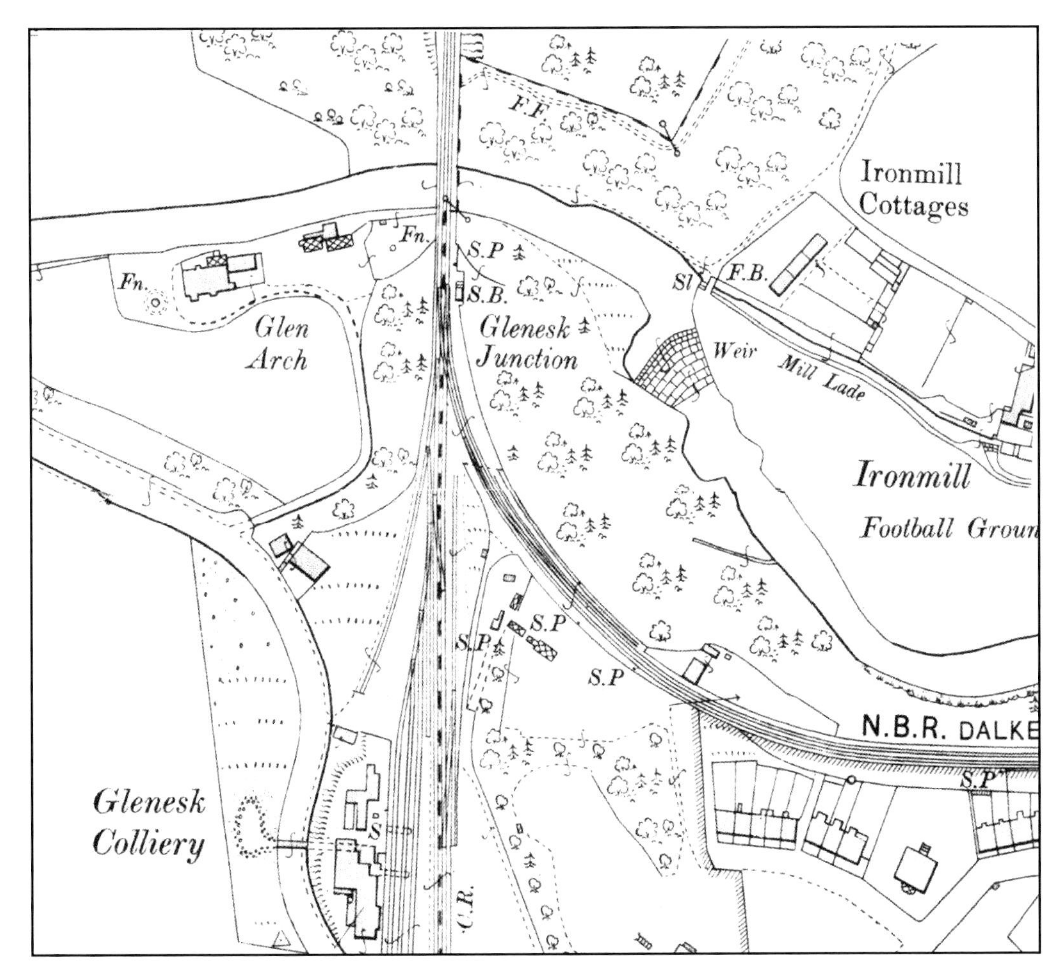

XXIV. Glenesk Junction was where the Dalkeith branch separated from the later Waverley route. The original line to Dalkeith opened as part of the Edinburgh & Dalkeith Railway and opened from the terminus at St. Leonards in Edinburgh in 1831. Construction of the new branch line beyond Glenesk to Dalkeith opened in 1839 and to south in stages eventually reaching Hawick in 1849. It ceased to be a junction when the goods yard at Dalkeith closed on 10th August 1964, the passenger service having succumbed in January 1942. Glenesk (or Elginhaugh) bridge is across the North Esk river (seen at the top of the map). It was restored to its original condition in 1993 and is one of Scotland's finest pre-Victorian railway bridges. The history around Glenesk Junction is complicated. The Edinburgh and Dalkeith Railway had a station, Lasswade Road, south of the junction which opened and closed in 1849. There was also a station, Glenesk, north of the Junction which openedin 1855 and closed completely in 1886. No photographs of these stations have been found. The Melville Coal Company sank a pit near the junction at Glen Esk to Dalkeith. In 1904 the NBR had an agreement for four sidings trailed into the down main line. Two sidings passed through the screens and two were for empty wagons. All were linked at the 'dead' end with a wagon traverse. The colliery was abandoned in August 1905. reopened in January 1919 (the same siding arrangement relaid) but was idle in 1923. The sidings were lifted except for one that became a public siding which lasted until 1956. 1907 map at 25" to 1 mile.

82. This is the first signal box at Glenesk Junction, north of the junction. The lady's shopping basket is on the Waverley line!! It was replaced on 7th October 1917 by the signal box seen in 83, south of the junction, which was itself closed on 1st October 1961. (R.W. Lynn coll.)

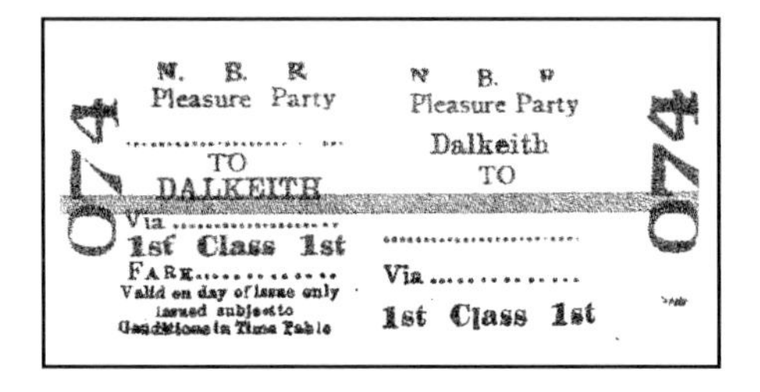

83. 0-6-0 Class J35 no.64479 passes Glenesk Junction on 21st April 1960 with a trip working to Dalkeith. Glenesk public siding is on the left. (W.S.Sellar)

DALKEITH

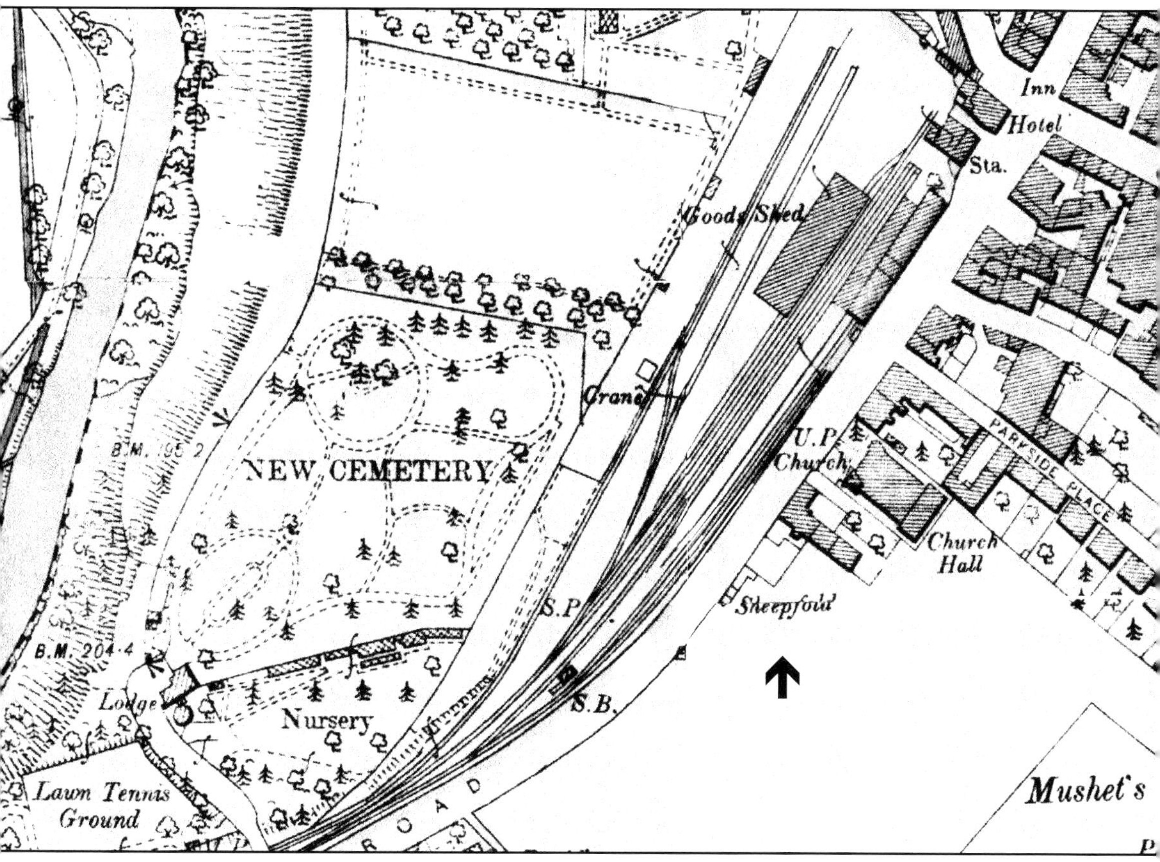

XXV. The original Edinburgh & Dalkeith Railway opened from St. Leonards, Edinburgh to serve the collieries around the town. With the opening of a new line from Hardengreen Junction to the pits on 31 July 1870, the line beyond the station was no longer required and removed. The branch terminus lost its passenger services on 9th January 1942 but goods traffic lasted until 10th August 1964. The station site was a bus depot and administrative offices for Eastern Scottish (later First Group) when the site was cleared for redevelopment. Since 1960 the population of Dalkeith has risen from 9,150 to 11,566 in 2011. 1893 map at 25" to 1 mile.

North British Main Line
DALKEITH.

A telegraph station.
HOTEL.—Cross Keys.
MARKET DAYS.—Monday and Thursday.
FAIRS—1st Thursday after Rutherglen May Fair, and 3rd Tuesday in October.

This burgh, is beautifully situated on the Esk river. *Dalkeith Palace*, the seat of the Duke of Buccleugh, was built by Ann, Duchess of Monmouth, on the site of the old castle, visited by Froissart, James VI., Charles I., who was a prisoner here, General Monk, who took it, George IV. in 1822, and Queen Victoria in 1848.

Extract from Bradshaw's Guide for 1866. (Reprinted by Middleton Press 2011)

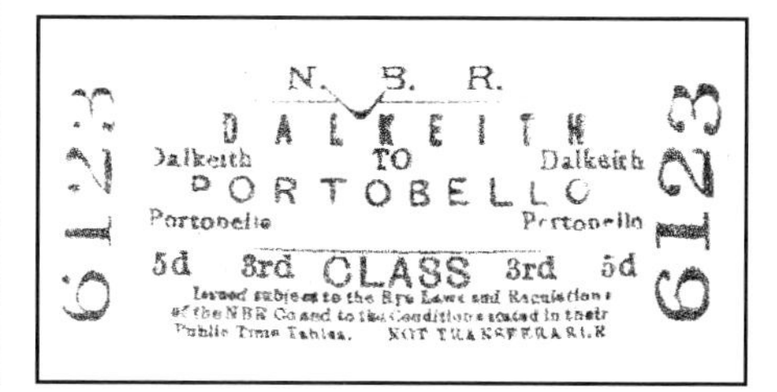

84. As we look towards the terminus, the goods shed can be seen in the centre and the platform on the right. The engine shed was located to the right of the platform alongside it. St.John's and Kings Park Church (Church of Scotland) is on the right. (N.E.Stead coll.)

85. A photograph taken in NBR days shows the long platform, the station buildings, dominant awning and the goods shed. The advert for the 'Scotsman' newspaper next to the nameboard was a common feature then. (W.R.Lynn coll.)

86. Taken nearer the buffer stops this 1930s view shows more of the large goods shed and the locomotive release points on to the passing loop enabling the branch locomotive to run round its train. Trains took 22 minutes to reach Edinburgh Waverley from here. (LOSA)

87. The Stephenson Locomotive Society (Scottish Area) organised a rail tour of lines around Edinburgh on 25th August 1962. The train was hauled by LNER designed V3 class 2-6-2T no.67668 which can be seen on the run round loop. (R.M.Casserley)

88. When the SLS visited Dalkeith, the track into the platform had already been removed. We can see open doors showing how the passengers descended to record the event for posterity. Health & Safety had not yet been invented! (R.M.Casserley)

DALKEITH ENGINE SHED

89. Dalkeith had a single road engine shed which opened on 7th July 1847 and closed in 1915. (R.W.Lynn coll.)

SHERRIFFHALL

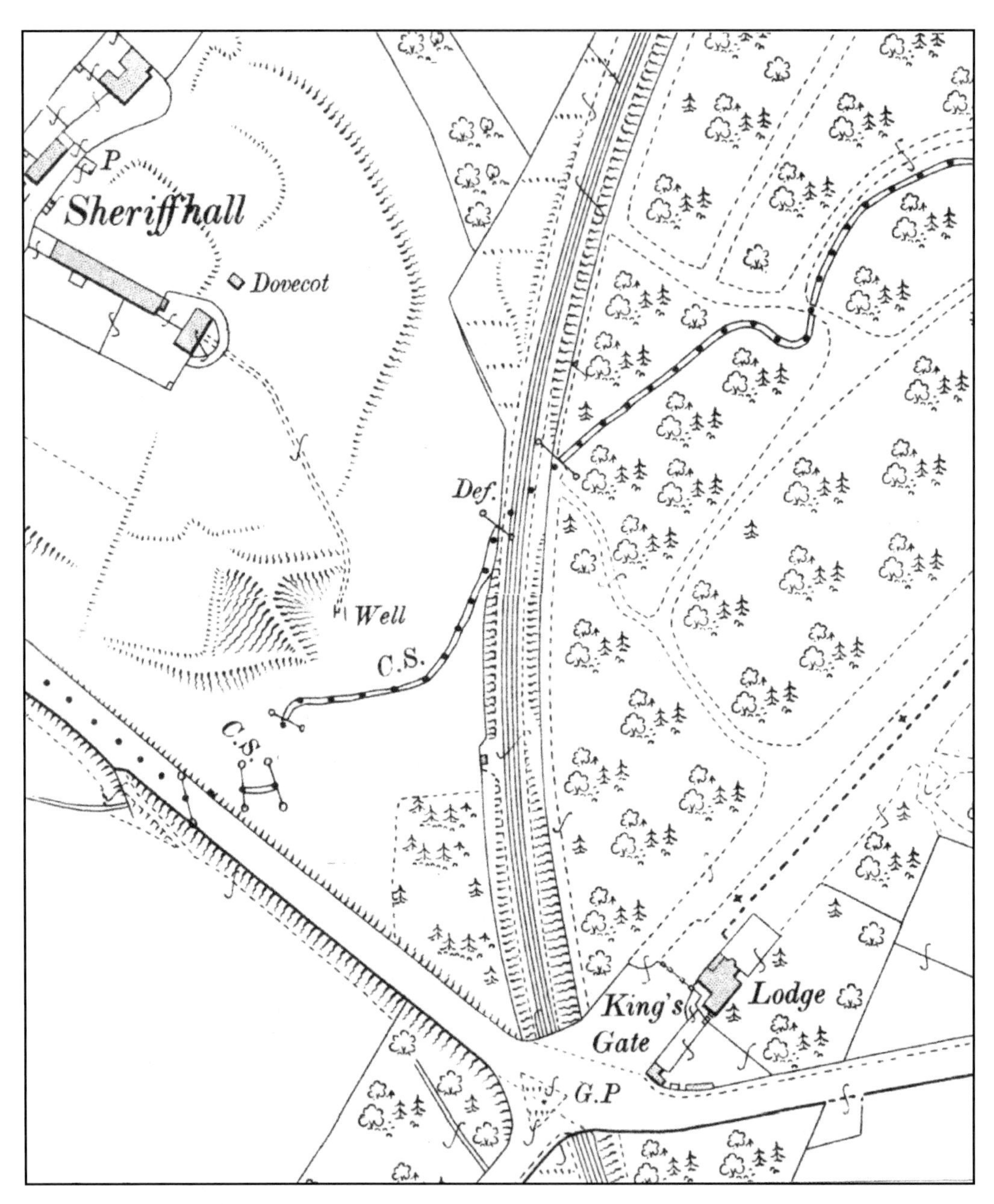

XXVI. Opened on 2nd June 1832 as part of the original Edinburgh & Dalkeith Railway the station's exact location is uncertain. We do know, however, that it was short lived and closed in June 1846. 1907 map at 25" to 1 mile.

MILLERHILL

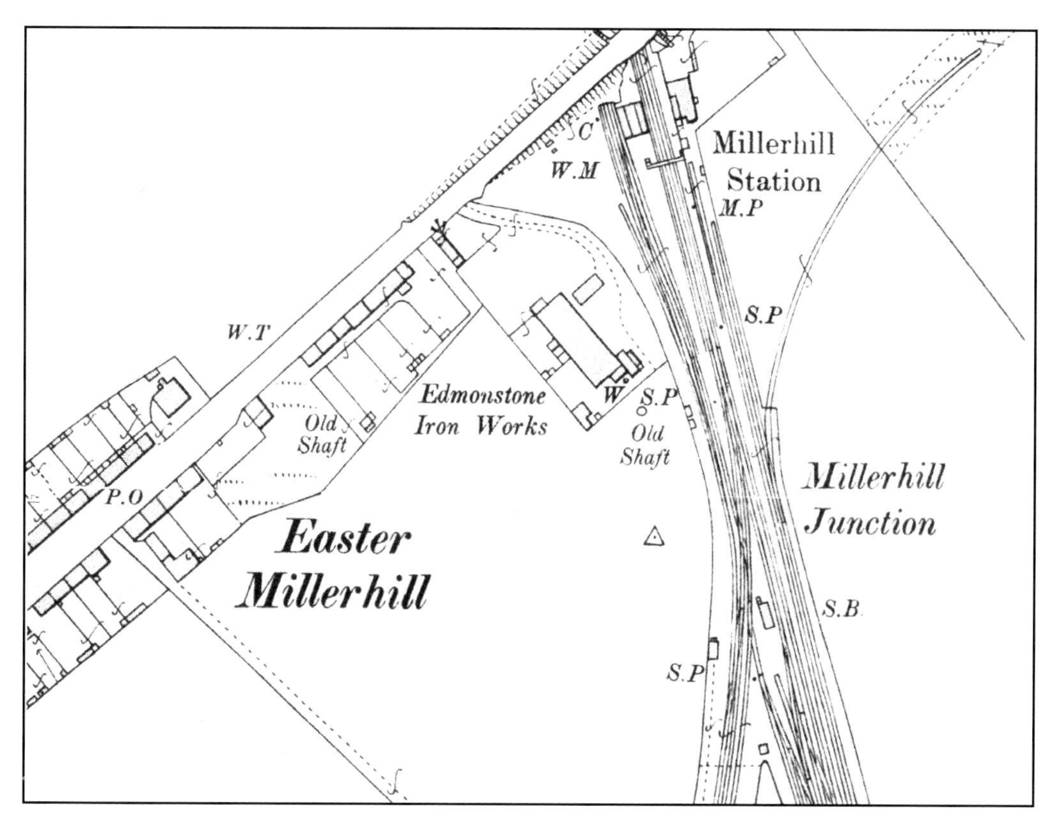

XXVII. Opened on 21st June 1847 the station closed to passenger traffic on 7th November 1955. From the same date the goods facilities became an unstaffed public siding before closing to traffic on 25th January 1965. The line emerging from the left at the bottom of the map is the Glencorse branch which was latterly retained to serve the now closed Bilston Glen Colliery. The track has recently been removed. The new Borders Railway will take a different alignment through Shawfair. 1908 map at 25" to 1 mile.

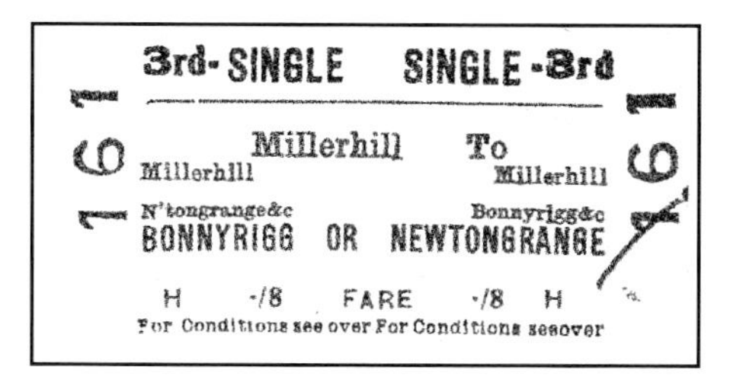

90. This view taken around 1912 shows a train approaching from Edinburgh whilst passengers and staff pose for the camera. The locomotive looks like a NBR Class D (LNER J33) 0-6-0. (LOSA)

91. This very regimented view was taken from the track. The platform edges have been rebuilt with concrete coping and the station now has electric lights.
(N.E.Stead coll.)

92. A similar view more safely taken. On the left, behind the nameboard, are the goods sidings.
(C.J.B. Sanderson/ARPT)

MILLERHILL MARSHALLING YARD

XXVII. Construction of a new marshalling yard to serve Edinburgh and allow closure of facilities in other locations began in 1958. It was built at a cost of £3m with the Up Yard opening on 18th June 1962 and the Down Yard on 20th May 1963. It was one of several constructed following publication of the British Railways Modernisation Plan in 1955. In line with the other yards built at the same time it has seen a major decline in traffic. The Down Yard closed on 27th November 1983 with the truncated Up Yard still in operation for remaining freight and engineers trains. Part of the Down Yard has been cleared of vegetation to provide the new alignment for the re-opened line from Tweedbank. The former turn-back siding used by trains terminating at Newcraighall has been rebuilt on to the new alignment ready to give access to works trains. The new alignment is necessary in order to serve the new community of Shawfair and also to pass under the Edinburgh City bypass. Millerhill Up Yard was opened on 18th June 1962, the Down Yard in April 1963. They replaced the yards at Hardengreen (Eskbank), Niddrie West, Joppa, Portobello and South Leith. The Meadows Yard (Seafield) had closed earlier on 29th September 1958.

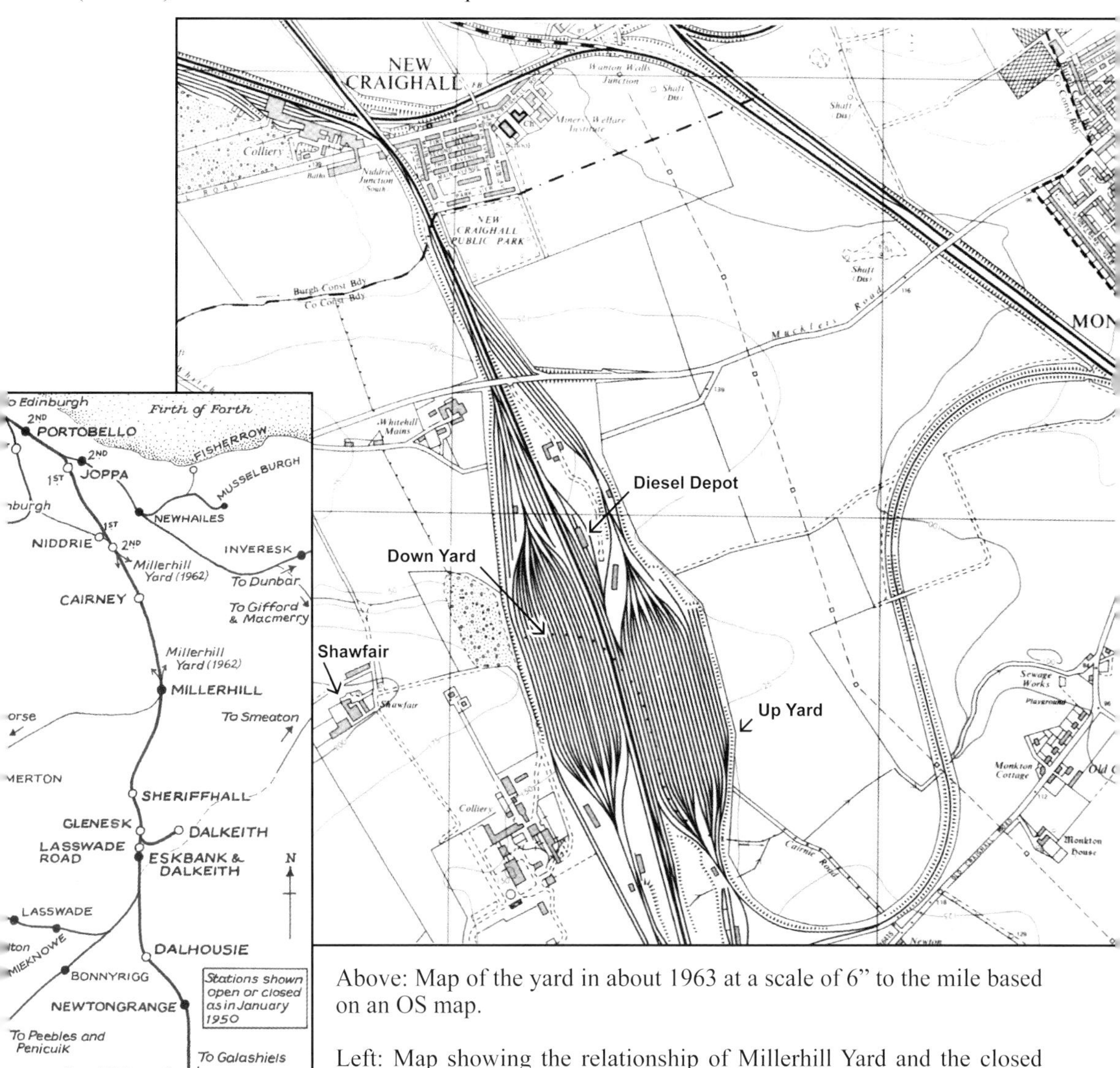

Above: Map of the yard in about 1963 at a scale of 6" to the mile based on an OS map.

Left: Map showing the relationship of Millerhill Yard and the closed stations of Millerhill, Cairney and Niddrie. (A.E.Young)

93. A Black 5 4-6-0 departs from Millerhill yard. The diesel depot can be seen above the train in the background. (S.Murdoch / Transport Treasury)

94. A3 class 4-6-2 no. 60100 *Spearmint* was seen passing Muckletts Bridge looking towards Monktonhall colliery whose buildings can be seen on the horizon above the locomotive. The A3 was getting ready to work a freight out of Millerhill. (A.P.McLean)

95. By 1963 both up and down yards were handling around 10,000 wagons each, per week. The up yard closed with the Waverley Route in 1969. By 1975 the throughput at the down yard was below 1000 wagons daily, so it was closed in November 1983. By 1986, the remnants of the up sidings had been relegated to a secondary marshalling yard. It remains so in 2013. This view taken on 17th June 1964 gives an indication of the size and complexity of the two yards which were separated by the Waverley route running through the middle of them. The up yard is on the left and the down yard is on the other side. (R.S.Carpenter)

96. The control tower still looks brand new on the 7th June 1964, the year after the completion of the entire complex. (R.S.Carpenter)

97. The start of work on the Waverley route seen here on 15th April 2011 when the turnback siding was moved onto cleared land which once housed the down yard at Millerhill to form the future route to Tweedbank. (D.A.Lovett)

MILLERHILL DIESEL DEPOT

98. This opened on 18th June 1962 with the new yard. Seven Class 17 Clayton locomotives with their distinctive centre cabs are stored alongside the still new looking depot on 19th June 1965. Two Class 08 diesel shunters stand in the distance by the fuel tanks. The steam era water tower looks out of place in the post modernisation plan era. (R.S.Carpenter)

99. A line up of class 40s and 37s alongside the single line maintenance shed at Millerhill on 3rd June 1978. Nearest the camera is no.40142 with no.37150 and no.40167 behind. (G.W.Morrison)

100. EWS Class 66/0 Co-Co DE nos.66182 and 66180 were on depot at Millerhill on 1st June 2000. Freight operator DB Schenker took it over when it acquired English, Welsh & Scottish Railway (EWS), who operated it after privatisation in 1994. (B.Morrison)

SOUTH OF NEWCRAIGHALL

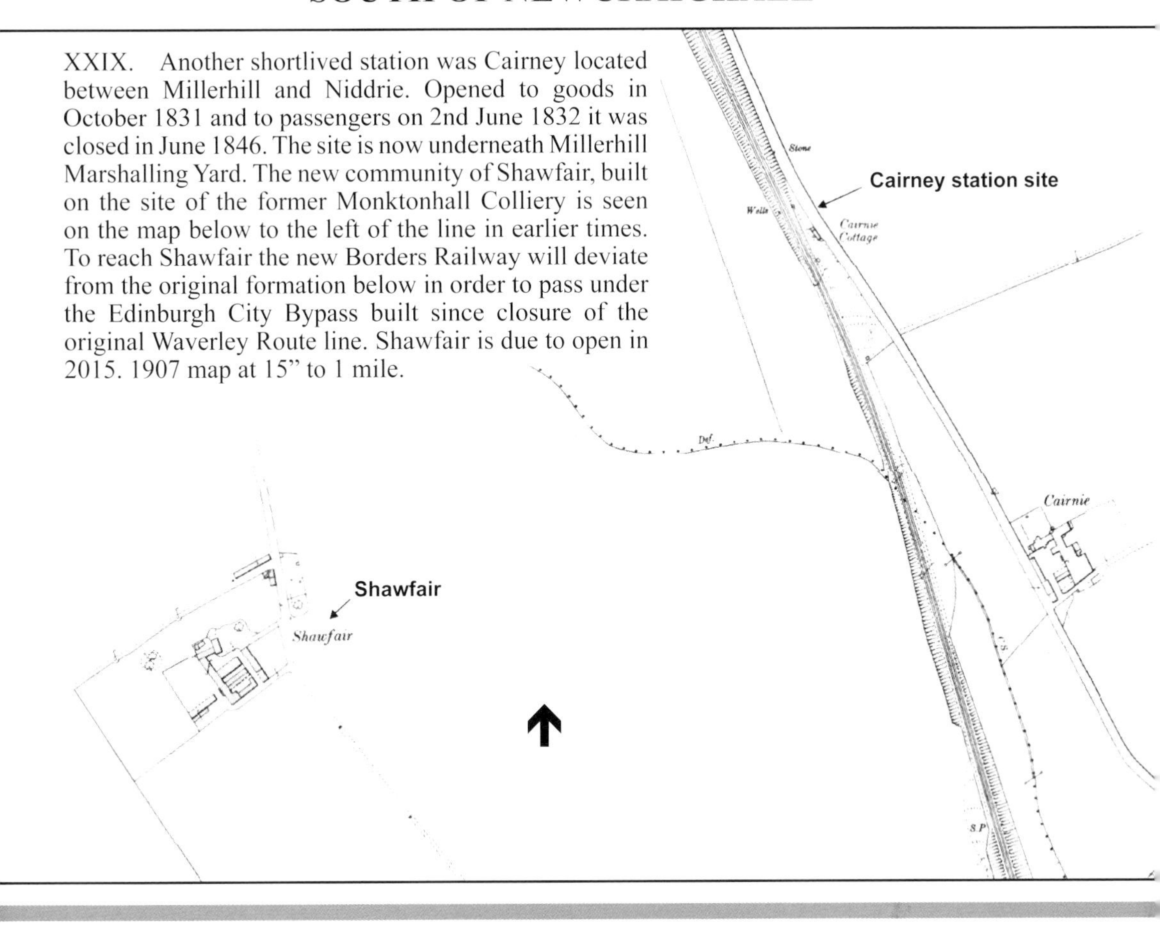

XXIX. Another shortlived station was Cairney located between Millerhill and Niddrie. Opened to goods in October 1831 and to passengers on 2nd June 1832 it was closed in June 1846. The site is now underneath Millerhill Marshalling Yard. The new community of Shawfair, built on the site of the former Monktonhall Colliery is seen on the map below to the left of the line in earlier times. To reach Shawfair the new Borders Railway will deviate from the original formation below in order to pass under the Edinburgh City Bypass built since closure of the original Waverley Route line. Shawfair is due to open in 2015. 1907 map at 15" to 1 mile.

NEWCRAIGHALL

101. The single line platform can be seen on the left under the bridge carrying the A1 road over the line. Seen here on 15th April 2011, the line on the right gives acess to and from what remains of Millerhill tard. The point on the left gives access to the passenger service turnback siding. (D.A.Lovett)

Newcraighall

102. Class 170 no. 170409 stands at the platform awaiting departure for Edinburgh and the north on 18th June 2009. Newcraighall was built on the site of the second Niddrie station and opened as part of the Edinburgh Crossrail scheme on 3rd June 2002. It is currently the terminus of the services to and from Fife. (D.A.Lovett)

103. Looking towards Millerhill, the A1 bridge can be seen at the end of the platform. The station is a park and ride and has a large car park and bus interchange. There are few passenger comforts apart from a small shelter and there are no booking office facilities tickets being bought either from machines or on the train. The station has recently been adopted by Portobello Rotary who have planted trees and encourage community use of the site. (D.A.Lovett)

NIDDRIE

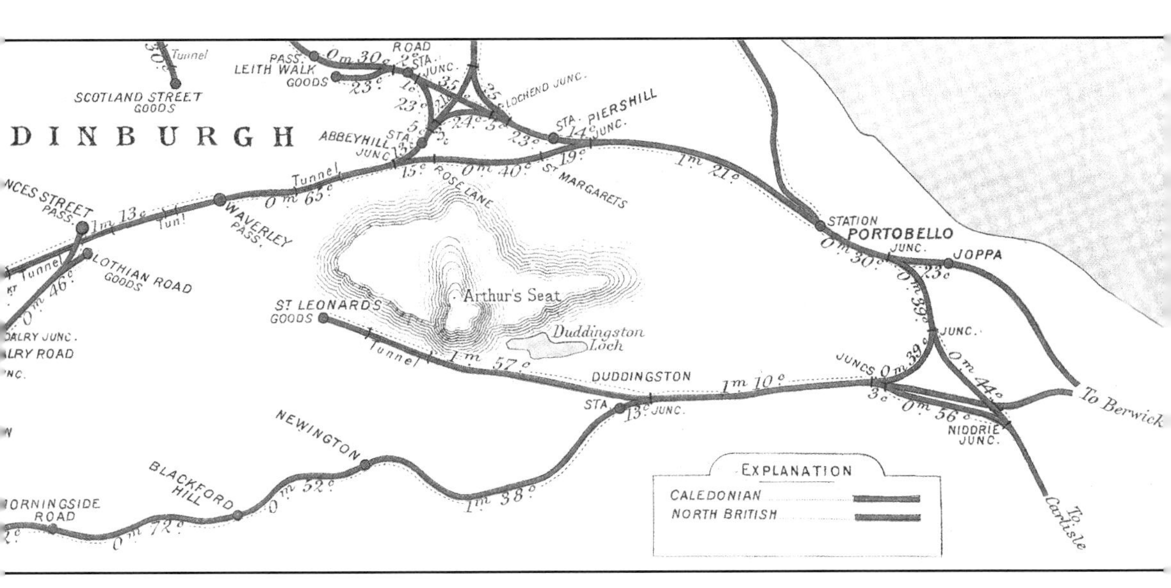

XXX. The first Niddrie station opened on 4th July 1831 and was known as Niddrie Junction. It had closed by October 1847 but was reopened for a brief period between 1st June and 1st October 1860. The second station opened on 1st December 1864 on a site to the north of the Junction but last appeared in Bradshaw in January 1869. The goods yard survived until 1950. The site of the second station is now occupied by Newcraighall station.

XXXI. Close up of the junctions at Niddrie and the goods station in 1895. 1895 map at 25" to 1 mile.

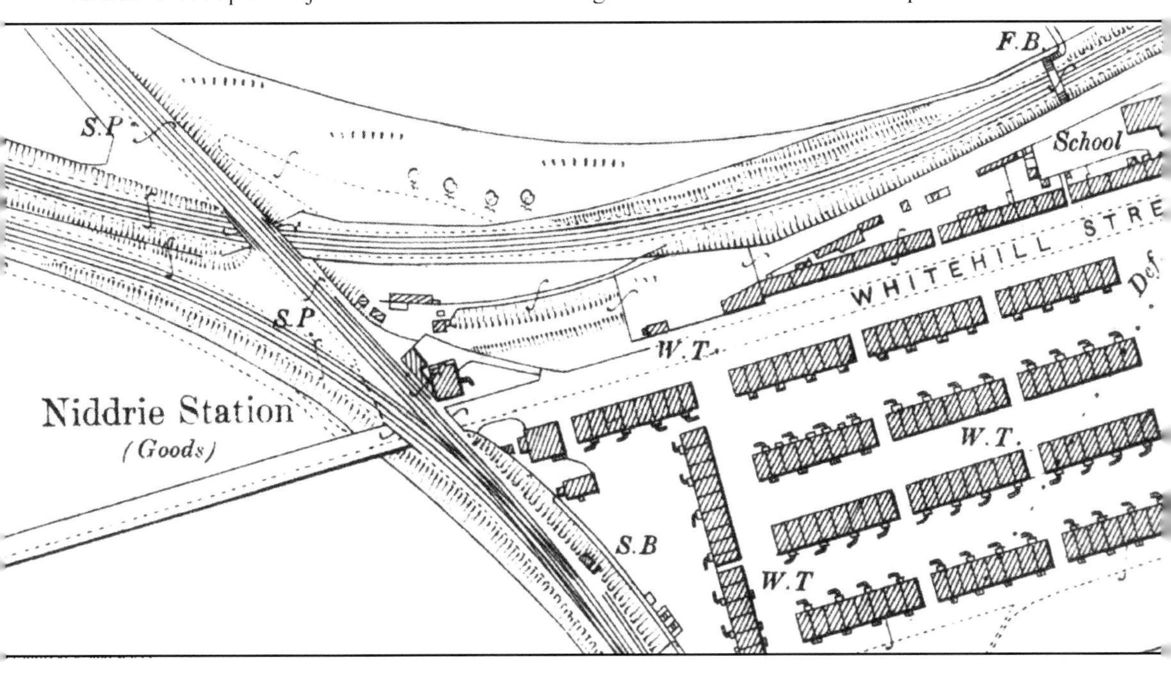

104. We are looking towards the site of the current Brunstane station with the Waverley Route on the right and the Edinburgh 'Sub' (Suburban) is on the left. The line over the top connected the East Coast Main Line to the Edinburgh 'Sub' at Niddrie West Junction. (R.W.Lynn coll.)

105. Viewed from the current Brunstane overbridge the electrified line to Millerhill is on the left and the Edinburgh 'Sub' line is on the right. The piers are those of the bridge which appears in 104. (D.A.Lovett)

BRUNSTANE

A station known as Joppa was established at Brunstane on 14th July 1847 but closed in 1859 when the second Joppa station was opened on the Edinburgh - Berwick main line. The present Brunstane was opened as part of the Edinburgh Crossrail scheme along with Newcraighall on 3rd June 2002. The line currently connects south Edinburgh with Fife after passing through Edinburgh Waverley. Tweedbank trains will call here in the future.

106. Class 158 no. 158711 approaches Brunstane from Edinburgh with a train for Newcraighall on 18th June 2009. (D.A.Lovett)

107. The single platform is on the electrified line to Millerhill Yard. This view from 18th June 2009 is looking towards the East Coast Main Line junction at Portobello.(D.A.Lovett)

PORTOBELLO

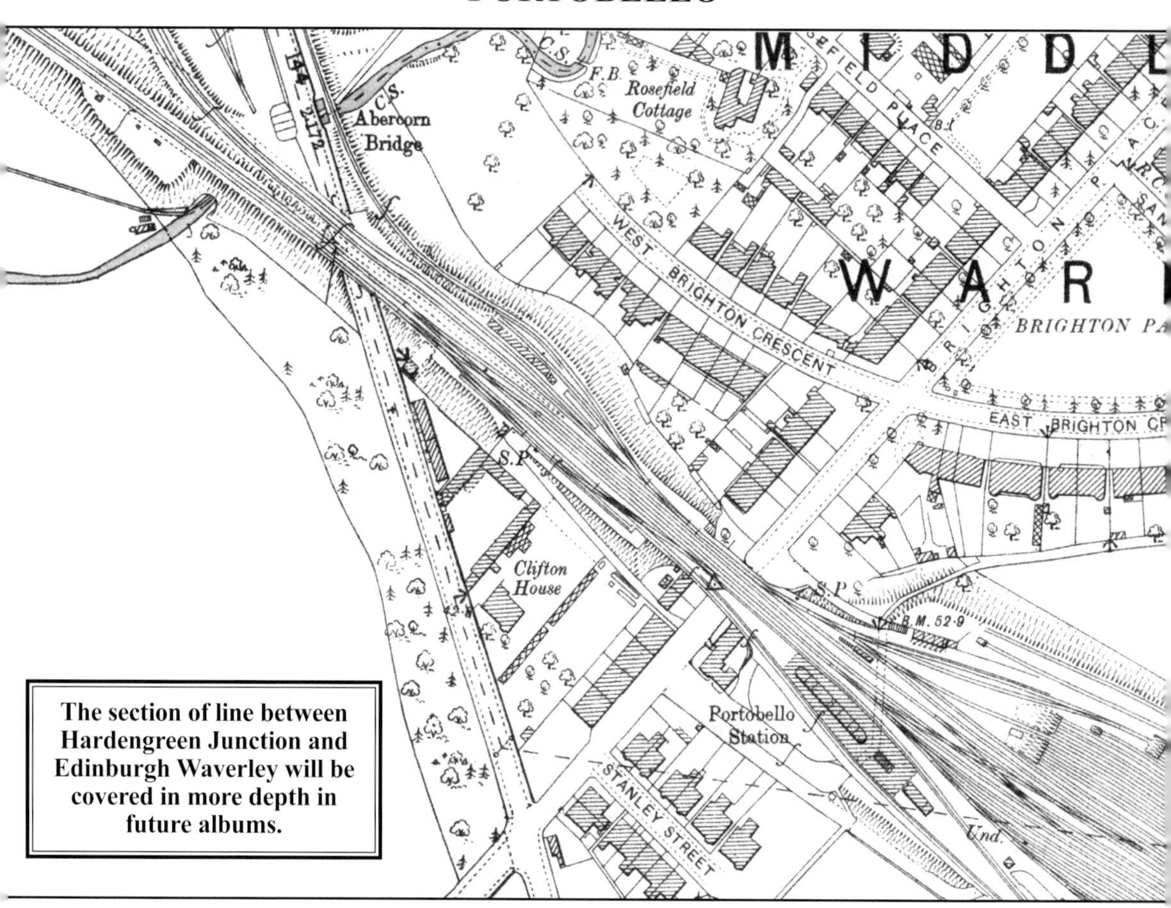

The section of line between Hardengreen Junction and Edinburgh Waverley will be covered in more depth in future albums.

XXXII. The first station at Portobello opened in March 1835 and was located at on the original route from St. Leonards to South Leith which was soon abandoned after the Edinburgh & Dalkeith Railway was taken over by the NBR. A replacement opened on the East Coast Main Line on 22nd June 1846, allowing the earlier station to close shortly afterwards on the 14th July. Portobello was Edinburgh's seaside resort and many outings were made from the Waverley route to enjoy a day by the coast. The Waverley route joined the East Coast Main Line at Portobello East Junction, the station being just beyond the junction, towards Edinburgh Waverley. The station closed on 7th September 1964, although the junction remained to serve Millerhill yard and after June 2002 the new stations on the Edinburgh Cross Rail route at Brunstane and Newcraighall. The first railway control office was opened at Portobello in 1913. It was situated in the former Portobello station used by Leith branch trains from 1858 to 1903. When District Control moved to Waverley, it became the yardmaster's office for Portobello marshalling yard until the 1960s. 1893 map at 25" to 1 mile.

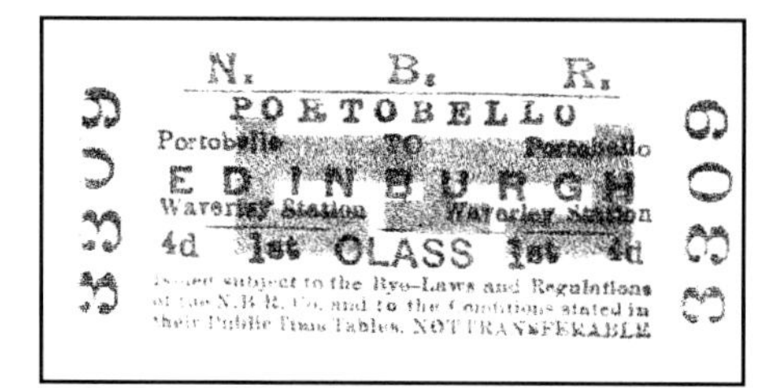

108. A1 Class 4-6-2 no. 60152 *Holyrood* approaches Portobello from Edinburgh Waverley with a local train. The locomotive was built in July 1949 and withdrawn from traffic in June 1965. (A.P.McLean)

109. On 29th August 1956, Haymarket allocated A4 Class 4-6-2 no. 60004 *William Whitelaw* hauls the up Glasgow Queen Street to London Kings Cross on to the Waverley Route at Portobello. The train was being diverted due to floods on the East Coast Main Line. Note the reversed headboard probably that of "The Elizabethan". (G.W.Morrison)

110. A DMU approaches Portobello from the south on 23rd August 1962. The plate girder bridge carrying the Lothian lines over the East Coast Main Line can be seen in the background. The Waverley Route diverges to the right.(C.J.B. Sanderson / ARPT)

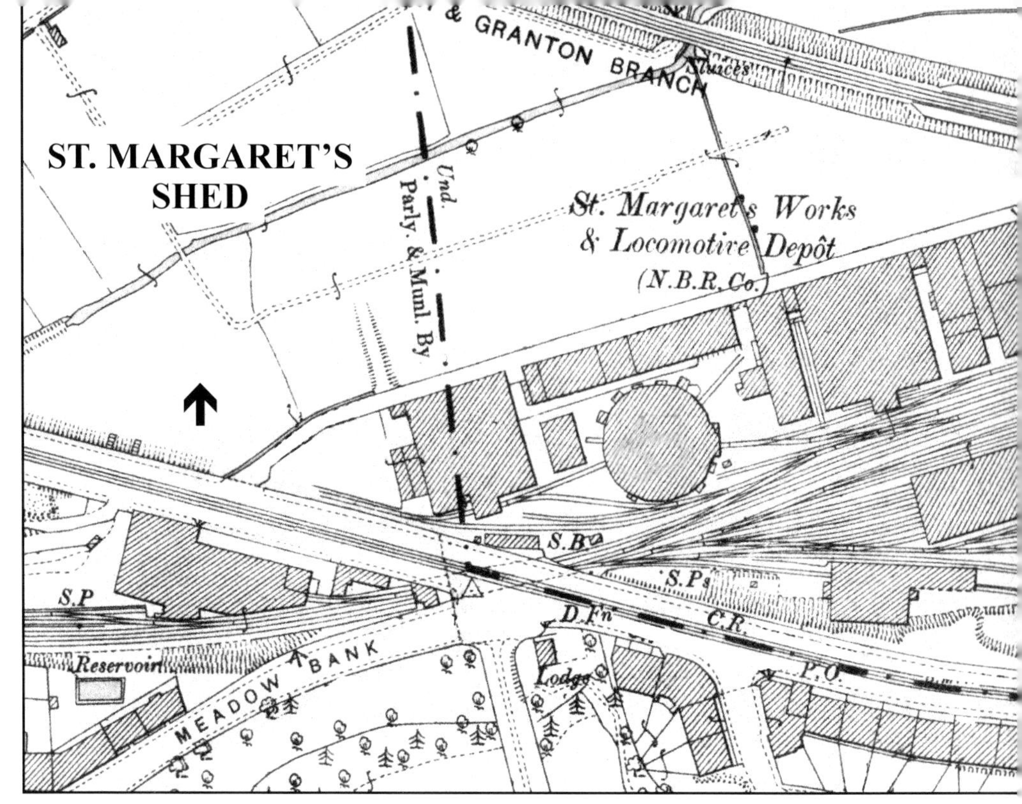

XXXIII. This was originally the site of the central workshops of the NBR. The works straddled the East Coast Main Line and repaired and maintained locomotives and rolling stock. The complex also housed the locomotive running shed which was initially a roundhouse opened on the Up (north) side which accepted the early locomotives built by contractors before the opening of the line. Thirty three locomotives were built at St. Margaret's between 1856 and 1859. After the NBR acquired the Edinburgh & Glasgow railway in August 1865, that company's works at Cowlairs, Glasgow, became the workshops of the enlarged NBR and St. Margaret's became a

111. Four Class Y9 shunting locomotives with LNER nos. 9042, 10095, 9010 and one other in the old roundhouse which is still standing but was roofless on 20th June 1937. (H.C.Casserley)

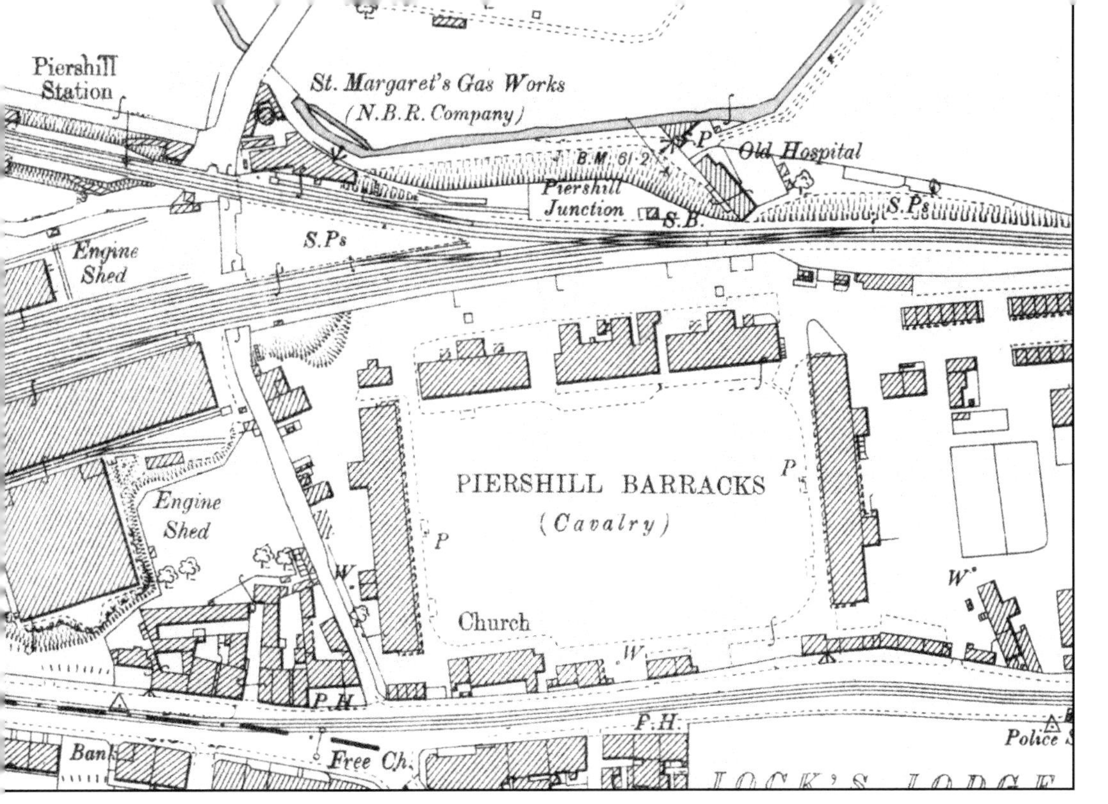

major locomotive running shed with the building of a six road running shed on the south side. Following the 1871 agreement with the NER which saw them assume responsibility for the haulage of Anglo-Scottish expresses between Berwick and Edinburgh, the NER opened its own shed on the Down side. As the facility was somewhat underused, the NBR agreed to use the surplus capacity. The arrangement ceased when both companies became part of the LNER on 1st January 1923. The depot at St. Margaret's closed on 1st May 1967 and part of the site was utilised for the construction of Meadowbank Stadium which was built to host the Commonwealth Games in 1970. 1895 map is at 15" to 1 mile.

112. A new six road running shed on the down side was provided in the 1860s to relieve pressure on the roundhouse on the up side which had opened in 1846. The NER also built a depot on the down side which was somewhat under utilised and was leased to the NBR until the Grouping in 1923. (R.S.Carpenter)

113. Surrounded by tenement buildings through the smoky atmosphere we can just about make out the six road shed and the coaling stage. This view is looking towards Portobello. (R.W.Lynn coll.)

114. The impressive entrance to the former roundhouse is just about standing in this view dated 17th May 1953. (R.S.Carpenter)

115. Y9 Class 0-4-0T no. 68102 stands in the yard at St. Margarets on 27th July 1958. Like most of these 'Pugs' it has a wooden tender. The tenement blocks on the main London Road (the A1) show how close the shed was to residential property. (ColourRail)

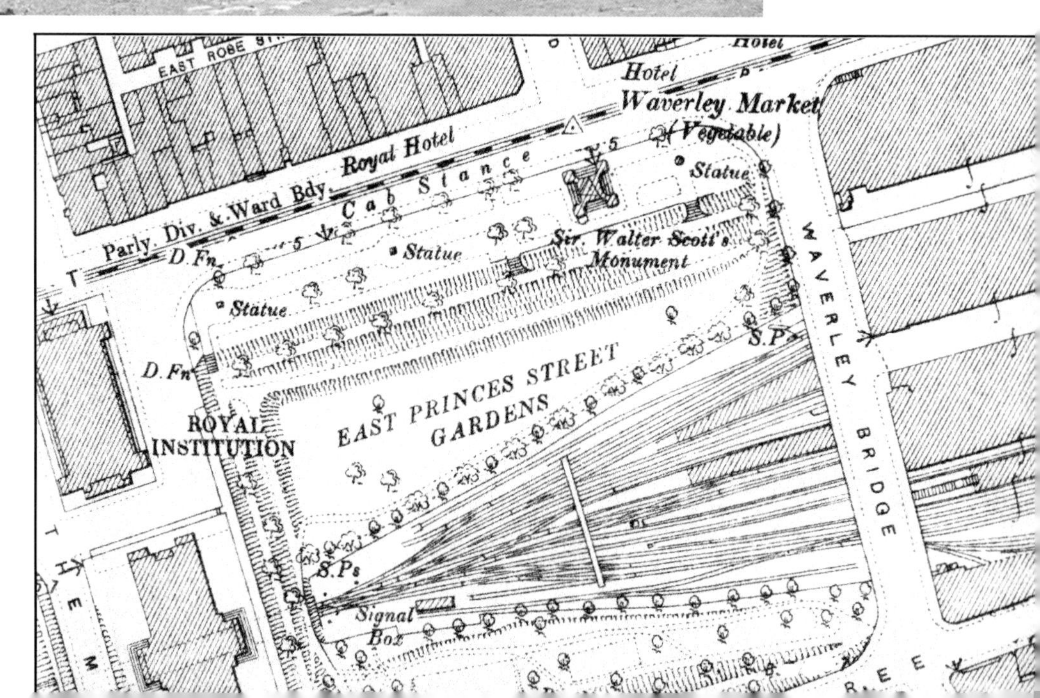

EDINBURGH WAVERLEY

XXXIV. At one time three separate stations occupied the site of the current Edinburgh Waverley. The first was known as North Bridge and opened with the original NBR line to Berwick on 22nd June 1846. These were subsequently joined by the opening of two new adjacent stations on 17th May 1847, Canal Street, the terminus of the Edinburgh, Leith & Newhaven Railway and the extension of the Edinburgh & Glasgow Railway from its original terminus at Haymarket into General station. With all three stations under North British Railway in 1865 the combined complex renamed Edinburgh Waverley in 1866. The station was extended between 1869 and 1873 with the removal of the market to the former Canal Street station site and the removal of Trinity Hospital and Trinity Church to new sites. On 5th August 1891 an Act of Parliament sanctioned the rebuilding of the station which included additional tunnels and quadrupling line from Corstophine in West Edinburgh to Abbeyhill Junction on the Berwick line. Rebuilding took place between 1892 and 1900. The through suburban platforms (20 & 21) opened on 17th April 1898. Covering 23 acres and 21 platforms the work cost £1.5m. The prestigious North British Hotel (now the Balmoral following its sale by British Rail in 1981) opened on 15th October 1902. Goods facilities were withdrawn on 2nd January 1967 and the site became the station car park. Network Rail completed in 2013 a major refurbishment of the station that started in 2006 and has restored it to its former glory. Today it serves a population of 430,082 and is one of the best known railway stations in the world. 1895 map at 15" to 1 mile.

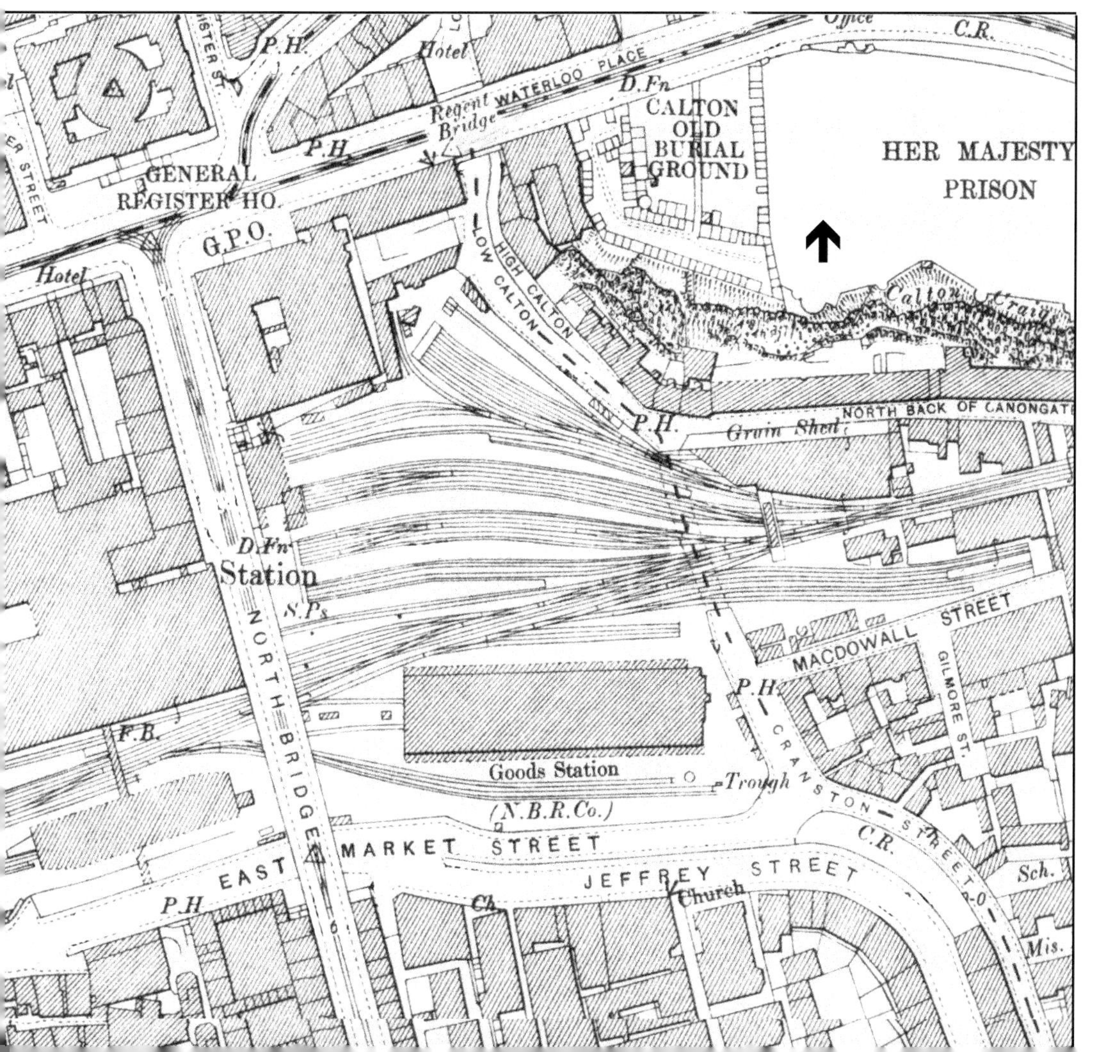

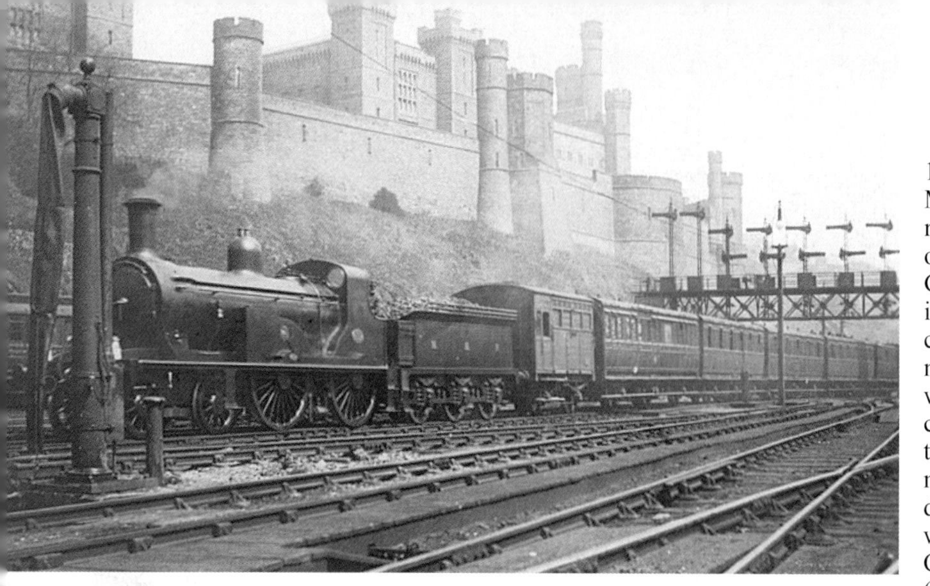

116 A NBR class M 4-4-0 no.312 arrives at Waverley on an express from Galashiels. Built in 1895 no.312 became LNER D31 no.9312 and was withdrawn in December 1938. At the time of the Grouping no.9312 was shedded at Blaydon for working the Border Counties line. (J.Alsop coll.)

117. D34 class 4-4-0 no.62490 *Glen Fintaig* arrives at Edinburgh Waverley on 25th July 1953, with a local service from North Berwick. (B.Morrison)

118. A4 class Pacific no. 60004 *William Whitelaw* departs from Edinburgh Waverley on 25th July 1953, hauling "The Elizabethan" for King's Cross. (B.Morrison)

119. The approach to Waverley is viewed in 1964 from the steps of Jacobs Ladder. The goods station is behind the signal box and the A4 class 4-6-2 awaiting the signal. The large building in the bottom left hand corner is New Street bus garage. (A.P.McLean)

120. An almost identical picture taken 45 years later on 18th June 2009 shows a much simplified track layout. The goods shed and yard have gone and the area accomodates the new Integrated Electronic Control Centre which replaced the former signal box. The bus garage has been demolished and the modern offices are those of Edinburgh City Council. (D.A.Lovett)

Easebourne Lane, Midhurst, West Sussex.
GU29 9AZ Tel:01730 813169

www.middletonpress.co.uk email:info@middletonpress.co.uk

A-978 0 906520 B- 978 1 873793 C- 978 1 901706 D-978 1 904474
E - 978 1 906008 F - 978 1 908174

All titles listed below were in print at time of publication - please check current availability by looking at our website - *www.middletonpress.co.uk* or by requesting a Brochure which includes our *LATEST* RAILWAY TITLES also our TRAMWAY, TROLLEYBUS, MILITARY and COASTAL series

A
Abergavenny to Merthyr C 91 8
Abertillery & Ebbw Vale Lines D 84 5
Aberystwyth to Carmarthen E 90 1
Allhallows - Branch Line to A 62 8
Alton - Branch Lines to A 11 6
Andover to Southampton A 82 6
Ascot - Branch Lines around A 64 2
Ashburton - Branch Line to B 95 4
Ashford - Steam to Eurostar B 67 1
Ashford to Dover A 48 2
Austrian Narrow Gauge D 04 3
Avonmouth - BL around D 42 5
Aylesbury to Rugby D 91 3

B
Baker Street to Uxbridge D 90 6
Bala to Llandudno E 87 1
Banbury to Birmingham D 27 2
Banbury to Cheltenham E 63 5
Bangor to Holyhead F 01 7
Bangor to Portmadoc E 72 7
Barking to Southend C 80 2
Barmouth to Pwllheli E 53 6
Barry - Branch Lines around D 50 0
Bartlow - Branch Lines to F 27 7
Bath Green Park to Bristol C 36 9
Bath to Evercreech Junction A 60 4
Beamish 40 years on rails E94 9
Bedford to Wellingborough D 31 9
Birmingham to Wolverhampton E253
Bletchley to Cambridge D 94 4
Bletchley to Rugby E 07 9
Bodmin - Branch Lines around B 83 1
Bournemouth to Evercreech Jn A 46 8
Bournemouth to Weymouth A 57 4
Bradshaw's Guide 1866 F 05 5
Bradshaw's History F18 5
Bradshaw's Rail Times 1850 F 13 0
Bradshaw's Rail Times 1895 F 11 6
Branch Lines series - see town names
Brecon to Neath D 43 2
Brecon to Newport D 16 6
Brecon to Newtown E 06 2
Brighton to Eastbourne A 16 1
Brighton to Worthing A 03 1
Bristol to Taunton D 03 6
Bromley South to Rochester B 23 7
Bromsgrove to Birmingham D 87 6
Bromsgrove to Gloucester D 73 9
Broxbourne to Cambridge F16 1
Brunel - A railtour D 74 6
Bude - Branch Line to B 29 9
Burnham to Evercreech Jn B 68 0

C
Cambridge to Ely D 55 5
Canterbury - BLs around B 58 9
Cardiff to Dowlais (Cae Harris) E 47 5
Cardiff to Pontypridd E 95 6
Cardiff to Swansea E 42 0
Carlisle to Hawick E 85 7
Carmarthen to Fishguard E 66 6
Caterham & Tattenham Corner B251
Central & Southern Spain NG E 91 8
Chard and Yeovil - BLs a C 30 7
Charing Cross to Dartford A 75 8
Charing Cross to Orpington A 96 3
Cheddar - Branch Line to B 90 9
Cheltenham to Andover C 43 7
Cheltenham to Redditch D 81 4
Chester Northgate to Manchester F 51 2
Chester to Birkenhead F 21 5
Chester to Rhyl E 93 2
Chester to Warrington F 40 6
Chichester to Portsmouth A 14 7
Clacton and Walton - BLs to F 04 8
Clapham Jn to Beckenham Jn B 36 7
Cleobury Mortimer - BLs a E 18 5
Clevedon & Portishead - BLs to D180
Consett to South Shields E 57 4
Cornwall Narrow Gauge D 56 2
Corris and Vale of Rheidol E 65 9
Craven Arms to Llandeilo E 35 2
Craven Arms to Wellington E 33 8
Crawley to Littlehampton A 34 5
Cromer - Branch Lines around C 26 0
Croydon to East Grinstead B 48 0
Crystal Palace & Catford Loop B 87 1
Cyprus Narrow Gauge E 13 0

D
Darjeeling Revisited F 09 3
Darlington Leamside Newcastle E 28 4
Darlington to Newcastle D 98 2
Dartford to Sittingbourne B 34 3
Denbigh - Branch Lines around F 32 1
Derwent Valley - BL to the D 06 7
Devon Narrow Gauge E 09 3
Didcot to Banbury D 02 9
Didcot to Swindon C 84 0
Didcot to Winchester C 13 0
Dorset & Somerset NG D 76 0
Douglas - Laxey - Ramsey E 75 8
Douglas to Peel C 88 8
Douglas to Port Erin C 55 0
Douglas to Ramsey D 39 5
Dover to Ramsgate A 78 9
Dublin Northwards in 1950s E 31 4
Dunstable - Branch Lines to E 27 7

E
Ealing to Slough C 42 0
Eastbourne to Hastings A 27 7
East Cornwall Mineral Railways D 22 7
East Croydon to Three Bridges A 53 6
Eastern Spain Narrow Gauge E 56 7
East Grinstead - BLs to A 07 9
East London - Branch Lines of C 44 4
East London Line B 80 0
East of Norwich - Branch Lines E 69 7
Effingham Junction - BLs a A 74 1
Ely to Norwich C 90 1
Enfield Town & Palace Gates D 32 6
Epsom to Horsham A 30 7
Eritrean Narrow Gauge E 38 3
Euston to Harrow & Wealdstone C 89 5
Exeter to Barnstaple B 15 2
Exeter to Newton Abbot C 49 9
Exeter to Tavistock B 69 5
Exmouth - Branch Lines to B 00 8

F
Fairford - Branch Line to A 52 9
Falmouth, Helston & St. Ives C 74 1
Fareham to Salisbury A 67 3
Faversham to Dover B 05 3
Felixstowe & Aldeburgh - BL to D 20 3
Fenchurch Street to Barking C 20 8
Festiniog - 50 yrs of enterprise C 83 3
Festiniog 1946-55 E 01 7
Festiniog in the Fifties B 68 8
Festiniog in the Sixties B 91 6
Ffestiniog in Colour 1955-82 F 25 3
Finsbury Park to Alexandra Pal C 02 8
Frome to Bristol B 77 0

G
Galashiels to Edinburgh F 52 9
Gloucester to Bristol D 35 7
Gloucester to Cardiff D 66 1
Gosport - Branch Lines around A 36 9
Greece Narrow Gauge D 72 2

H
Hampshire Narrow Gauge D 36 4
Harrow to Watford D 14 2
Harwich & Hadleigh - BLs to F 02 4
Hastings to Ashford A 37 6
Hawick to Galashiels F 36 9
Hawkhurst - Branch Line to A 66 6
Hayling - Branch Line to A 12 3
Hay-on-Wye - BL around D 92 0
Haywards Heath to Seaford A 28 4
Hemel Hempstead - BLs to D 88 3
Henley, Windsor & Marlow - BLa C77 2
Hereford to Newport D 54 8
Hertford & Hatfield - BLs a E 58 1
Hertford Loop E 71 0
Hexham to Carlisle D 75 3
Hexham to Hawick F 08 6
Hitchin to Peterborough D 07 4
Holborn Viaduct to Lewisham A 81 9
Horsham - Branch Lines to A 02 4
Huntingdon - Branch Line to A 93 2

I
Ilford to Shenfield C 97 0
Ilfracombe - Branch Line to B 21 3
Industrial Rlys of the South East A 09 3
Ipswich to Saxmundham C 41 3
Isle of Wight Lines - 50 yrs C 12 3
Italy Narrow Gauge F 17 8

K
Kent Narrow Gauge C 45 1
Kidderminster to Shrewsbury E 10 9
Kingsbridge - Branch Line to C 98 7
Kings Cross to Potters Bar E 62 8
Kingston & Hounslow Loops A 83 3
Kingswear - Branch Line to C 17 8

L
Lambourn - Branch Line to C 70 3
Launceston & Princetown - BLs C 19 2
Lewisham to Dartford A 92 5
Lines around Wimbledon B 75 6
Liverpool Street to Chingford D 01 2
Liverpool Street to Ilford C 34 5
Llandeilo to Swansea E 46 8
London Bridge to Addiscombe B 20 6
London Bridge to East Croydon A 58 1
Longmoor - Branch Lines to A 41 3
Looe - Branch Line to C 22 2
Lowestoft - BLs around E 40 6
Ludlow to Hereford E 14 7
Lydney - Branch Lines around E 26 0
Lyme Regis - Branch Line to A 45 1
Lynton - Branch Line to B 04 6

M
Machynlleth to Barmouth E 54 3
Maesteg and Tondu Lines E 06 2
Majorca & Corsica Narrow Gauge F 41 3
March - Branch Lines around B 09 1
Marylebone to Rickmansworth D 49 4
Melton Constable to Yarmouth Bch E031
Midhurst - Branch Lines of E 78 9
Midhurst - Branch Lines to F 00 0
Minehead - Branch Line to A 80 2
Mitcham Junction Lines B 01 5
Mitchell & company C 59 8
Monmouth - Branch Lines to E 20 8
Monmouthshire Eastern Valleys D 71 5
Moretonhampstead - BL to C 27 7
Moreton-in-Marsh to Worcester D 26 5
Mountain Ash to Neath D 80 7

N
Newbury to Westbury C 66 6
Newcastle to Hexham D 69 2
Newport (IOW) - Branch Lines to A 26 0
Newquay - Branch Lines to C 71 0
Newton Abbot to Plymouth C 60 4
Newtown to Aberystwyth E 41 3
North East German NG D 44 9
Northern Alpine Narrow Gauge F 37 6
Northern France Narrow Gauge C 75 8
Northern Spain Narrow Gauge E 83 3
North London Line B 94 7
North Woolwich - BLs around C 65 9
Nottingham to Lincoln F 43 7

O
Ongar - Branch Line to E 05 5
Orpington to Tonbridge B 03 9
Oswestry - Branch Lines around E 60 4
Oswestry to Whitchurch E 81 9
Oxford to Bletchley D 57 9
Oxford to Moreton-in-Marsh D 15 9

P
Paddington to Ealing C 37 6
Paddington to Princes Risborough C819
Padstow - Branch Line to B 54 1
Pembroke and Cardigan - BLs to F 29 1
Peterborough to Kings Lynn E 32 1
Plymouth - BLs around B 98 5
Plymouth to St. Austell C 63 5
Pontypool to Mountain Ash D 65 4
Pontypridd to Merthyr F 14 7
Pontypridd to Port Talbot E 86 4
Porthmadog 1954-94 - BLa B 31 2
Portmadoc 1923-46 - BLa B 13 8
Portsmouth to Southampton A 31 4
Portugal Narrow Gauge E 67 3
Potters Bar to Cambridge D 70 8
Princes Risborough - BL to D 05 0
Princes Risborough to Banbury C 85 7

R
Reading to Basingstoke B 27 5
Reading to Didcot C 79 6
Reading to Guildford A 47 5
Redhill to Ashford A 73 4
Return to Blaenau 1970-82 C 64 2
Rhyl to Bangor F 15 4
Rhymney & New Tredegar Lines E 48 2
Rickmansworth to Aylesbury D 61 6
Romania & Bulgaria NG E 23 9
Romneyrail C 32 1
Ross-on-Wye - BLs around E 30 7
Ruabon to Barmouth E 84 0
Rugby to Birmingham E 37 6
Rugby to Loughborough F 12 3
Rugby to Stafford F 07 9
Ryde to Ventnor A 19 2

S
Salisbury to Westbury B 39 8
Sardinia and Sicily Narrow Gauge F 50 5
Saxmundham to Yarmouth C 69 7
Saxony Narrow Gauge D 47 0
Seaton & Sidmouth - BLs to A 95 6
Selsey - Branch Line to A 04 8
Sheerness - Branch Line to B 16 2
Shenfield to Ipswich E 96 3
Shrewsbury - Branch Line to A 86 4
Shrewsbury to Chester E 70 3
Shrewsbury to Crewe F 48 2
Shrewsbury to Ludlow E 21 5
Shrewsbury to Newtown E 29 1
Sierra Leone Narrow Gauge D 28 9
Sirhowy Valley Line E 12 3
Sittingbourne to Ramsgate A 90 1
Slough to Newbury C 56 7
South African Two-foot gauge E 51 2
Southampton to Bournemouth A 42 0
Southend & Southminster BLs E 76 5
Southern Alpine Narrow Gauge F 22 2
Southern France Narrow Gauge C 47 5
South London Line B 46 6
South Lynn to Norwich City F 03 1
Southwold - Branch Line to A 15
Spalding - Branch Lines around E
Stafford to Chester F 34 5
St Albans to Bedford D 08 1
St. Austell to Penzance C 67 3
St. Boswell to Berwick F 44 4
Steaming Through Isle of Wight A
Steaming Through West Hants A
Stourbridge to Wolverhampton E
St. Pancras to Barking D 68 5
St. Pancras to Folkestone E 88 8
St. Pancras to St. Albans C 78 9
Stratford-u-Avon to Birmingham D
Stratford-u-Avon to Cheltenham C
Sudbury - Branch Lines to F 19 2
Surrey Narrow Gauge C 87 1
Sussex Narrow Gauge C 68 0
Swanley to Ashford B 45 9
Swansea - Branch Lines around F
Swansea to Carmarthen E 59 8
Swindon to Bristol C 96 3
Swindon to Gloucester D 46 3
Swindon to Newport D 30 2
Swiss Narrow Gauge C 94 9

T
Talyllyn 60 E 98 7
Taunton to Barnstaple B 60 2
Taunton to Exeter C 82 6
Taunton to Minehead F 39 0
Tavistock to Plymouth B 88 6
Tenterden - Branch Line to A 21 5
Three Bridges to Brighton A 35 2
Tilbury Loop C 86 4
Tiverton - BLs around C 62 8
Tivetshall to Beccles D 41 8
Tonbridge to Hastings A 44 4
Torrington - Branch Lines to B 37
Towcester - BLs around E 39 0
Tunbridge Wells BLs A 32 1

U
Upwell - Branch Line to B 64 0

V
Victoria to Bromley South A 98 7
Victoria to East Croydon A 40 6
Vivarais Revisited E 08 6

W
Walsall Routes F 45 1
Wantage - Branch Line to D 25 8
Wareham to Swanage 50 yrs D09
Waterloo to Windsor A 54 3
Waterloo to Woking A 38 3
Watford to Leighton Buzzard D 45
Welshpool to Llanfair E 49 9
Wenford Bridge to Fowey C 09 3
Westbury to Bath B 55 8
Westbury to Taunton C 76 5
West Cornwall Mineral Rlys D 48
West Croydon to Epsom B 08 4
West German Narrow Gauge D 93
West London - BLs of C 50 5
West London Line B 84 8
West Wiltshire - BLs of D 12 8
Weymouth - BLs A 65 9
Willesden Jn to Richmond B 71 8
Wimbledon to Beckenham C 58 1
Wimbledon to Epsom B 62 6
Wimborne - BLs around A 97 0
Wisbech - BLs around C 01 7
Witham & Kelvedon - BLs a E 82
Woking to Alton A 59 8
Woking to Portsmouth A 25 3
Woking to Southampton A 55 0
Wolverhampton to Shrewsbury E4
Worcester to Birmingham D 97 5
Worcester to Hereford D 38 8
Worthing to Chichester A 06 2
Wrexham to New Brighton F 47 5
Wroxham - BLs around F 31 4

Y
Yeovil - 50 yrs change C 38 3
Yeovil to Dorchester A 76 5
Yeovil to Exeter A 91 8
York to Scarborough F 23 9